THE MAUDSLEY

Maudsley Monographs

MAUDSLEY MONOGRAPHS

HENRY MAUDSLEY, from whom the series of monographs takes its name, was the founder of The Maudsley Hospital and the most prominent English psychiatrist of his generation. The Maudsley Hospital was united with the Bethlem Royal Hospital in 1948 and its medical school, renamed the Institute of Psychiatry at the same time, became a constituent part of the British Postgraduate Medical Federation. It is now associated with King's College, London, and entrusted with the duty of advancing psychiatry by teaching and research. The Bethlem-Maudsley NHS Trust, together with the Institute of Psychiatry, are jointly known as The Maudsley.

The monograph series reports work carried out at The Maudsley. Some of the monographs are directly concerned with clinical problems; others, less obviously relevant, are in scientific fields that are cultivated for the furtherance of psychiatry.

Editor
Professor Sir David Goldberg MA DM MSc FRCP FRCPsych DPM
Assistant Editors
Professor A S David MPhil MSc FRCP MRCPsych MD
Dr T Wykes BSc PhD MPhil

Previous Editors

1955-1962	Professor Sir Aubrey Lewis LLD DSc MD FRCP and Professor G W Harris MA MD DSc FRS
1962-1966	Professor Sir Aubrey Lewis LLD DSc MD FRCP
1966-1970	Professor Sir Denis Hill MB FRCP FRCPsych DPM and Professor J T Eayrs PhD DSc
1970-1979	Professor Sir Denis Hill MB FRCP FRCPsych DPM and Professor G S Brindley MD FRCP FRS
1979-1981	Professor G S Brindley MD FRCP FRS and Professor G F M Russell MD FRCP FRCP(ED) FRCPsych
1981-1983	Professor G F M Russell MD FRCP FRCP(ED) FRCPsych
1983-1989	Professor G F M Russell MD FRCP FRCP(ED) FRCPsych and Professor E Marley MA MD DSc FRCP FRCPsych DPM
1989-1993	Professor G F M Russell MD FRCP FRCP(ED) FRCPsych and Professor B H Anderton BSc PhD

Maudsley Monographs number thirty-nine

Aggression
Individual differences, alcohol, and benzodiazepines

Alyson J. Bond, BA, MSc, PhD
Senior Lecturer and Chartered Clinical Psychologist,
Institute of Psychiatry, University of London

Malcolm H. Lader, DSc, PhD, MD,
FRCPsych
Professor of Clinical Psychopharmacology,
Institute of Psychiatry, University of London

Jose Carlos C. da Silveira, MD
Federal University of Minas Gerais/UFMG, Brazil

Psychology Press
a member of the Taylor & Francis group

Psychology Press Ltd., Publishers
27 Church Road
Hove
East Sussex, BN3 2FA
UK

British Library Cataloguing in Publication Data

A catalogue record for this book is available from the British Library

    ISBN 0-86377-482-2
    ISSN 0076-5465

Printed and bound in the UK by TJ Press (Padstow) Ltd.

Contents

Acknowledgements

We are indebted to Professor John Gunn and Dr. Paul Bowden of the Department of Forensic Psychiatry, Institute of Psychiatry, Maudsley Hospital, for invaluable advice on some of the clinical aspects of the study and for referral of the patients studied. We are also grateful to Professor Isaac Marks and Professor Stuart Checkley for allowing us to test some of their patients. We should like to thank Mrs. Lily Hughes for her careful typing of the manuscript. Finally we should like to thank all who participated as subjects in these experiments.

This research was supported by the Medical Research Council of the UK and by a scholarship to Dr. da Silveira from the Conselho Nacional de Desenvolvimento Cientifico e Tecnológico-CNPq Brazil.

Preface

Aggression as a behaviour and hostility as a feeling state are an increasing problem in many parts of the world including the UK. Although much has been written about these phenomena, relatively few studies have attempted to analyse the behavioural, affective and cognitive components, nor to relate these to physiological responses accompanying the feeling of hostility or the behavioural repertoire of aggression. In particular, attempts to set up paradigms of aggressive behaviour in the psychological laboratory have been progressing slowly.

Our own interest in the topic stems from several sources. First, our studies on anxiety, an emotion in response to stimuli perceived as threatening, overlapped inevitably with aggression as a complementary or alternative response. Second, our contact with psychiatric patients in our various clinics led to a practical concern with hostility as a primary aspect of these patients. Third, our psychopharmacological studies, especially of depressants such as alcohol and the benzodiazepines, caused us to address the specific issue of the effects of these drugs on hostility and aggression.

To that end, we adopted and adapted a laboratory model of aggression based on a competitive reaction-time task. Several studies have been completed but we have selected two clinical and three psychopharmacological studies as exemplars of the insight that can be obtained using psychological, psychophysiological, and psychopharmacological techniques in a multi-disciplinary approach. Part of this work formed the basis of a PhD thesis submitted to the University of London by J.C.C. da Silveira.

Alyson Bond
Malcolm Lader
Jose Carlos da Silveira
London, June 1996

CHAPTER ONE

The psychology of aggression

In this chapter, definitions and theories of aggressive behaviour are discussed. Several factors are important in aggressive behaviour and these are discussed under three broad headings: interpersonal factors, external factors, and individual differences.

TERMINOLOGY

Aggression is a word that in ordinary language encompasses a wide range of behaviours. However, these sometimes diverse behaviours seem to have a common thread and the aim of a psychological definition is to explain this. There have been many definitions of aggression. For example, Harre and Lamb (1983, p.13) catalogued more than 250. These various definitions seem to share the idea that aggression involves inflicting harm or damage but beyond this, there are a number of differences. For example, does the damage have to be inflicted on a living creature or does damage to objects or property also count as aggression? Does the damage have to be physical as argued by Zillman (1978) or does psychological harm such as saying something hurtful or damaging someone's reputation also constitute an aggressive act? Given that these distinctions may be important, one solution is to define aggression broadly but then describe different types of aggression. This approach

1

has been taken by Buss (1961) who said aggression could be physical or verbal, active or passive, direct or indirect. Combining these factors yields eight types of aggression altogether.

Another issue, perhaps less easily resolved, concerns whether the damage or harm must be inflicted intentionally for the act to be considered aggressive. On the one hand it seems desirable to exclude inflicting harm accidentally, e.g. accidentally hitting someone with an object or saying something tactless without thinking. On the other hand, intentions cannot be observed and it may cause problems to use a definition that rests on unobservable behaviour. This was the view of Buss (1961) and Bandura (1973) whose definitions ignore the intentions that may lie behind the "response that delivers noxious stimuli to another organism". Despite these difficulties, many authors have included intention in their definitions of aggression. For example, Dollard, Doob, Miller, Mowrer, and Sears (1939) defined aggression as "an act whose goal-response is injury to an organism". Berkowitz (1974) also argues that intention is crucial. This was taken up by Geen (1976) whose working definition can be summarised in three points: (1) "Aggression consists of the delivery of noxious stimuli by one organism to another"; (2) "The stimuli are delivered by the former with the intent to harm the latter"; (3) "The one delivering the stimuli expects that the probability of the stimuli reaching the source is greater than zero". Note that this definition does not specify any particular emotional state, such as anger, or any particular attitude towards the victim, such as dislike or hostility. It does specify intention to harm but this should not be taken to exclude other intentions or motives.

This definition then implies that aggression is a form of social interaction in which the perpetrator intends to harm the victim in some way. Baron (1977) also proposes that the victim must be motivated to avoid such treatment in order to exclude sado-masochistic behaviour. Aggressive behaviour may also be classified into subtypes.

AFFECTIVE AND INSTRUMENTAL AGGRESSION

Behaviours characterised as aggressive may have different antecedents and intervening processes. Thus, aggressive behaviours are different from each other with respect to what motivates them, although they may be accommodated heuristically under the terms of affective or hostile and instrumental (cf. Baron, 1977). "Affective" aggression is that accompanied by a strong negative emotional state (see Table 1.1). In this

TABLE 1.1
Characteristics of different types of aggression

Affective	*Instrumental*
Hostile	Goal-directed
Primary intent to harm	Coercive power
Strong negative emotional state	Military
Provoked	Obedience to authority
Annoyance-motivated	Incentive-motivated
Reactive	Proactive

case an intervening process—anger—instigates and guides the aggressive behaviour of which the main goal is injury or harm to the provocateur (Feshbach, 1964). Johansson (1981) lists its main characteristics: activation of the hypothalamus, increased blood flow to the musculature, heightened blood pressure and pulse rate, pupillary dilatation and decreased flow of blood to the viscera. Anger is inferred as a necessary but not sufficient condition—its presence does not inevitably produce affective aggression. However, the closeness between anger and the actual aggressive behaviour sometimes reinforces the idea of a cause–effect relationship.

Another type of aggression has been dubbed by Tedeschi (1984) "instrumental", and is related to behaviour whose main goal is not intent to harm but to establish social and coercive power over others through aggressive means. In this case, an aggressive option has been judged as most likely to be successful in achieving a favourable outcome to a conflict of interests. This form of aggression may occur when people defend property or rights and is found in war and social conflicts: Following a command from a person in authority some peaceful individuals are capable of committing extreme acts of violence (Milgram, 1963). Bandura (1973) argues that both affective and instrumental aggression are directed towards the attainment of specific goals and are therefore instrumental. As a result of this, other terms have been coined (see Table 1.1). Zillmann (1979) refers to annoyance-motivated and incentive-motivated. Dodge and Coie (1987) have proposed the terms reactive and proactive. Reactive aggression concerns retaliation to a perceived threat, whereas proactive aggression is used to obtain some other goal, e.g. dominance. However, an aggressive act often has elements of both types.

THEORETICAL PERSPECTIVES

Having defined aggressive behaviour, we now need to consider the reasons why it occurs. Many theoretical perspectives exist but Baron and Richardson (1994) divide them into four categories, which we will briefly discuss.

Aggression as an instinct

According to the theories of instinctive aggression, aggression occurs because humans are genetically programmed for such behaviour. These theories have generally arisen from animal work and assume that aggression provided biological advantages to our prehistoric ancestors. Lorenz (1966) proposed an evolutionary perspective. He suggested that the aggressive instinct is a source of energy that builds up over time and needs to be discharged. The greater the amount of energy accumulated, the weaker the stimulus necessary for overt aggression to occur. Freud (1920) also proposed that aggression stemmed from an innate, self-directed death instinct (*thanatos*) that is turned outward towards destruction of others. Both these theories regarded aggression as inevitable: The energy would build up until it could be released in some way either to attain the original goal or in some form of displacement activity. Lorenz believed that aggressive energy could be dispersed by many minor hostile but noninjurious acts, thus decreasing the likelihood of violent outbursts. According to instinctive theories, aggression is an unavoidable, integral part of human nature.

Aggression as a drive

The theories of aggression as a drive assume that it is a motivational force induced by some kind of deprivation to terminate or reduce that state. This perspective was elaborated by Dollard et al. (1939) in the frustration–aggression hypothesis: "aggression is always a consequence of frustration and, contrariwise, that the existence of frustration always leads to some form of aggression". Frustration, i.e. the blocking of some form of goal-directed behaviour, induces an aggressive drive, which facilitates aggressive behaviour. This theory initially gained widespread support but it eventually faltered on the certainty of both premises. First, the tenet that frustration always leads to aggression has been challenged by many empirical studies showing that frustration may lead to numerous alternative responses, e.g. despair. Thus, Miller (1941) refined the model to include other possible forms of behaviour. Second, there is much evidence that aggression may occur as a result of factors other than frustration. Indeed, frustration does not seem necessary for instrumental aggression such as self-defence.

Berkowitz (1974) further modified the drive theory to include contextual cues. He still accepted frustration as an important antecedent for aggressive behaviour but stressed the role of mediating factors in the environment. He therefore postulated that frustration led to negative affect or anger but this only led to aggression in the presence of aggressive cues. Both people and objects may become aggressive cues by previous association with anger arousal.

Cognitive models

The instinctive and drive theories of aggression ignore both emotion and cognition. Newer theories have attempted to revise the frustration theory to include these important elements. Thus, Berkowitz (1989) revised his earlier theory to state that frustration or other aversive stimuli (external factors) instigate aggressive reactions by creating negative affect. The response would then be determined by the individual's interpretation of the negative affect. If it was interpreted as anger, then aggressive tendencies would be likely to be aroused and more attention might be paid to aggressive cues. This was termed the "cognitive neoassociation model".

Zillman (1988) argued that cognition and excitation (arousal) are truly interdependent. Under very high levels of excitation, there may be interference with the cognitive processes that inhibit aggression, leading to impulsive aggression. At moderate levels of excitation, cognitive processes would operate to reduce aggression. In the same way, in a normal state of arousal, cognitions about an event are likely to influence the extent of arousal. If mitigating circumstances are recognised, there is likely to be a decay of any excitation. According to cognitive theories, people might be able to reduce aggressive behaviour by learning new ways of coping with provocation.

Social learning models

In contrast to aggression perceived as an instinct or a drive, Bandura (1977) has postulated that aggressive behaviour is acquired and maintained in a similar way to other forms of social behaviour. He does not discount biological or motivational factors, but postulates that the specific form, frequency, location, and target of aggressive behaviour are largely determined by social learning. Thus, reinforcing or rewarding aggressive behaviour increases the likelihood of repetition. Although direct experience may be important, work on children has shown observation and imitation (modelling) to be very influential. Bandura has suggested that there are three principal sources of aggressive models: the family, the subculture, and the mass media. If we observe aggressive behaviour being rewarded and we identify with the aggressor, we are more likely to use it ourselves. We may in fact learn new (aggressive) ways of responding. This behaviour can, however, be modified by self-imposed consequences. Thus, habitually aggressive people may reward themselves for successful intimidation of others, whereas people who disapprove of aggressive behaviour may experience guilt if they behave in the same way. Social learning theory then suggests that aggression only occurs under appropriate social conditions and we can change these conditions to reduce it.

INTERPERSONAL FACTORS IN AGGRESSION

Aggressive behaviour occurs within an interactive situation. Several possible behaviours may occur in an interpersonal exchange and therefore much research has been devoted to examining the conditions that facilitate an aggressive response. These studies have focused on frustration, provocation, attack, and instigation from others.

Frustration
Frustration, defined as the thwarting by one individual of another's goal-directed behaviour, has been assumed to be a strong elicitor of aggressive behaviour since the original hypothesis (Dollard et al., 1939). A large number of experiments seem at first to confirm that frustration is indeed an important antecedent of aggression. However, Baron and Richardson (1994) have pointed out that frustration has often been confounded by other factors in these early investigations. Studies that have carefully isolated different antecedents do confirm that frustration is one important factor in the induction of aggression (Berkowitz & Geen, 1967; Burnstein & Worchel, 1962). In one study it was shown that both frustration and personal insult increased aggression (Geen, 1968). Moreover, frustration did not need to be a result of the actions of others. Subjects who became frustrated through their own inability to accomplish a task also showed more aggression.

Other studies have found that frustration does not necessarily lead to an aggressive response (Buss, 1966; Kuhn, Madsen, & Becker, 1967). In these studies no differences were found between the frustrated and control groups. Together these studies cast some doubts on the early formulations that frustration is always a cause for aggression. Perhaps even more surprising than these results, however, is the suggestion in several additional experiments (Gentry, 1970; Rule & Hewitt, 1971) that exposure to strong frustration may sometimes serve to reduce rather than enhance later aggression. Frustration may elicit behaviours other than aggressive ones that attenuate the connection between frustration and aggression (cf. Buss, 1961). Barker, Dembo, and Lewin (1941, cf. Buss, 1961) contend that frustration may also produce useless, maladaptive, or regressive behaviour. Mandler (1972) argues that helplessness and anxiety, not aggression, may follow as a consequence of a person's response to feeling frustrated. Thus, the sequence of behaviours would depend on the subject's understanding of the responses that are available.

The current position seems to be that frustration sometimes facilitates aggression depending on certain factors. Baron and Richardson (1994) cite four important mediating factors: the magnitude; the presence of aggressive cues; the extent to which it is arbitrary or unexpected; and the emotional and cognitive processes of the frustrated individual. Frustration can be increased by intervening when the subject is close to his or her goal, by blocking expectation of success, and by making the subject's reasons for the action less legitimate (Harris, 1974; Kulick & Brown, 1979). Berkowitz (1989) has argued that frustration only produces a readiness for aggressive behaviour. The occurrence will depend on the presence of aggressive cues, i.e. stimuli associated with anger arousal. Such cues may be heightened by viewing violent films. Frustration that can be predicted or expected rarely produces aggression. However, if it is seen to be arbitrary or unjustified, it is more likely to result in aggressive behaviour. As well as aggressive cues, Berkowitz (1989) has emphasised the current feelings of the individual. Interpersonal or external factors that lead to negative affect or irritation increase the likelihood of aggressive behaviour.

In his reformulation of the relationship between frustration and aggression, Berkowitz (1989) discerns an associative network between negative affects, frustration, and aggression. In his model, the intensity and arbitrariness of the frustration leads to negative affect, and then aggressive cues may intensify the instigation to aggress. Attributions and judgements may facilitate or inhibit this process.

Provocation and attack

Attack is the key instigator to retaliatory aggression. Interpersonal aggression takes place in an interactive situation between two people. Therefore Bandura (1973, p.153) suggests that "if one wished to provoke aggression, the most dependable way to do so would be simply to physically assault another person, who would then be likely to oblige with a vigorous counterattack". Many studies support this idea. Persons who have been insulted or physically attacked are likely to respond with verbal abuse (James & Mosher, 1967), or with physical counterattack (Baron, 1972; Berkowitz, 1974). Moreover, the intensity of aggression depends on the intensity of the initiating attack (Epstein & Taylor, 1967;

O'Leary & Dengerink, 1973). Verbal provocation can often lead on to aggressive actions. In research examining police reports of criminal violence, Felson (1982, 1984) found a typical pattern to start with an insult leading to verbal retaliation, escalating to an argument, threats, and finally physical assault. This work emphasises the interactive nature of aggression. Several investigators have compared frustration (blocking of ongoing behaviour) with attack (delivery of noxious stimulus) as antecedents of aggression (e.g. Buss, 1963; Geen, 1968; Geen & Berkowitz, 1967). They conclude that attack is a more effective manoeuvre in eliciting aggression. Diamond et al. (1984) have also shown that attack is a more powerful source of arousal than is frustration. Baron (1977), however, argues that although frustration seems to be a weaker stimulus for aggression than either physical or verbal attack, comparable outcomes between the two variables have sometimes been misleading due to the ignorance of the subjective effects of each on the individual. The relevant question is whether or not a mild insult would always be more effective in eliciting subsequent aggression than extremely strong frustration. Somewhat more unexpected, however, is evidence that individuals often react aggressively to indications of aggressive intention on the part of others, even when they are not actually attacked by these persons. Greenwell and Dengerink (1973) found experimentally that although attack is an important instigator of aggressive behaviour, symbolic elements that are incorporated in that attack may play a major role.

These results have received support from many other empirical studies. Epstein and Taylor (1967) also showed that intent to harm is in fact a more powerful determinant of retaliation than is the absolute intensity of an attack. Dodge, Murphy, and Buchsbaum (1984) showed that subjects tend to be more aggressive when they perceive a hostile intention in the other party, whether or not the person is actually hostile. The absence of malice or lack of intention in the attacker constrains victims not to retaliate (Johnson & Rule, 1986; Zillmann & Cantor, 1976). The role of perceived intentionality in aggression also seems to be influenced by personality characteristics (Dodge, 1980). Attribution of hostile intent by aggressive boys, even in ambiguous circumstances, has been explained by Nasby, Hayden, and DePaulo (1979) as a consequence of a hostile attributional bias resulting from a generally aggressive disposition.

A factor related to the relationship between attack and aggression is that of apology. Schwartz, Kane, Joseph, and Tedeschi (1978) and Darby and Schlenker (1982) studied the belief that apologies can mitigate a victim's anger and aggression. These authors found that the subjects tended to judge the transgressors as less liable to punishment if they made apologies. Schlenker and Darby (1981) suggested that people tend to use a more complex apology involving a larger number of components as the harm gets more serious. When the harm is severe, they argue, more intense apologies may be needed to alleviate the conditions of the victims. It seems likely that the severity of harm may in some way control the inhibitory effects of apologies on aggression.

Instigation from others

Aggression may not just be an interaction between two people. The presence of others may influence behaviour. This may be either by emphasising restraint or conversely by encouraging increased aggression. This is related to anticipated approval or disapproval of onlookers (Borden, 1975). Figures of authority have much more power to influence events. Many acts of aggression, especially those carried out by the police or armed forces, stem from commands from superiors, not from provocation or frustration. Obedience to these figures of authority may not be surprising because such figures have the support of society at large. However, some influential research has shown that even a relatively powerless source of authority can induce individuals to be very aggressive. Milgram (1974) conducted a series of well-known experiments and found that the majority of people (65%) were prepared to punish a supposed learner with increasingly painful shocks when instructed to do so. Two factors seem to be effective in counteracting this obedience: First, having to take responsibility for your own actions, and second, exposure to disobedient models.

EXTERNAL FACTORS IN AGGRESSION

Various adverse environmental factors may increase the likelihood of aggression, e.g. heat, noise, crowding, pollution. However, Bandura (1973) claims that this is only true when such behaviour represents a dominant behavioural tendency. When other responses are dominant, then adverse conditions may inhibit aggression. Much laboratory work has attempted to elucidate the relationship between excessive heat and aggression. These investigations have in fact indicated that the relationship is curvilinear. The chance of aggression increases as negative affect (induced by high temperatures) rises only up to a certain point. After this point is reached, the likelihood of aggression decreases as other responses such as escape from the situation dominate (Baron & Bell, 1976). Unfortunately this relationship is not supported by archival studies. In these a significant linear relationship is demonstrated between increasing temperature, violent crime, and other aggressive behaviour. It is likely that this relationship is much more complex, e.g. hot weather encouraging more people on to the streets and more consumption of alcohol, leading to the possibility of more aggression.

Noise seems to have a clearer relationship to aggression than temperature. Laboratory studies using loud and unpleasant noise have found that it facilitates the occurrence of aggression (Geen, 1978; Mueller, 1983). This especially applies when the noise is unpredictable or uncontrollable.

Work on overcrowding originated in studies of animals where a link with aggressive behaviour has been found. Although there is evidence that both high population density and crowding may be perceived as unpleasant and stressful to humans, there is no clear link to increased aggression. Another environmental factor is air pollution with smoke, solid wastes, and noxious gas. Laboratory studies have revealed that subjects required to breathe secondary cigarette smoke were more aggressive to the experimenter regardless of his behaviour to them (Zillman, Baron, & Tamborini, 1981). Other forms of air pollution may be more associated with malodour. An experiment investigating the effects of unpleasant odour (Rotton, Frey, Barry, Milligan, & Fitzpatrick, 1979) found more effects on aggression when it was moderately unpleasant than when it was extremely obnoxious. It is likely then that malodour is similar to temperature in having a curvilinear effect. The likelihood of aggression may decrease when the source of discomfort can be clearly identified and when escape becomes the dominant response.

As well as environmental factors, other external components may contribute to aggressive behaviour. A substantial body of work has linked violence in the mass media to aggressive feelings and behaviour. Several studies have found that viewing violent as opposed to nonviolent films increases aggressive behaviour on a task afterwards (e.g. Geen & O'Neal, 1969). This work has been criticised as lacking a no-film control. It has been claimed that viewing a nonviolent film may actually lower aggression compared to not seeing a film. Zillman and Johnson (1973) investigated this hypothesis and found that viewing a neutral, nonviolent film did lower aggression compared to both a violent film and no-film conditions. Berkowitz (1984) suggests that media effects are due to aggressive cues resulting in priming. If people are asked to list thoughts after viewing various films, they produce more aggressive thoughts as their rating of the level of violence increases (Bushman & Geen, 1990). Although much research has investigated the facilitating effects of violence shown in the media and a positive relationship has been found between watching television violence and aggression in adolescence, it is important to recognise that people who habitually display aggressive behaviour also show an increased preference for viewing violence (Huesmann & Eron, 1986; Wartella, 1995). Violence in the media may also increase the autonomic arousal of the viewer. Increased arousal may strengthen any responses, one of which may be aggression depending on cues, or it may be aversive to the subject leading to negative mood, which may be interpreted as anger, which in turn may be a precursor to aggressive behaviour.

Pain may also serve as an external factor increasing the likelihood of aggression. The prime goal may be escape but where this is blocked it may lead to aggression. Berkowitz (1983) proposed that pain generates negative affect in a similar way to heat and that this may facilitate an aggressive response.

Substance use is a common factor in aggression of varying degrees of severity. Habitual alcohol and drug use has been reported for repeat murderers (Adler & Lidberg, 1995; Tiihonen & Hakola, 1994). Both alcohol use and aggression have shared antecedents such as family pathology and childhood experiences of neglect or abuse (Fagan, 1990; White, Brick, & Hansell, 1993), which could partially account for such a relationship. However, in nonclinical populations, alcohol use is often reported prior to violent crime (Collins & Schlenger, 1988). Therefore, both acute and chronic use of alcohol has been shown to contribute to increased aggression. Laboratory research has confirmed this association (Bushman & Cooper, 1990) but has indicated that the relationship is complex, both contextual cues and individual characteristics being important. Further discussion of the effects of alcohol can be found in Chapters 5 and 6.

Arousal, cognition, and anger

Many external variables may lead to increased arousal, which may be cognitively interpreted as anger. These processes may be described as intervening variables between the provoking stimulus and the aggressive response. Aggressive behaviour itself may also be associated with activation of the sympathetic nervous system leading to physiological arousal expressed in bodily symptoms. Arousal increases the probability of aggressive behaviour under certain conditions. It has been argued (Berkowitz, 1969) that frustration and provocation lead to a state of arousal that in turn energises aggressive responses that the person is disposed to make. Arousal, however, contributes to aggression not only by energising responses. Its combination with specific thoughts generated within the situation can create a state of increased anger, which predisposes the person to aggression. Schachter and Singer's general two-factor theory of emotion (1962) is the original proposition of this idea. According to their model, a central determinant of how individuals behave is the way in which they label a state of heightened physiological arousal as an affective experience.

The link between physiological arousal and emotion is reducible to three propositions: (1) when an individual has no immediate physiological explanation for a state of physiological arousal, s/he will label the state and describe her/his feelings according to the cognitions available to her/him; (2) when the individual has a completely appropriate explanation for her/his physiological arousal, no evaluative needs will arise and the individual will label her/his feelings accordingly; (3) the individual will react emotionally and will report emotions only to the extent that s/he experiences the state of physiological arousal. The widely cited experiment (Schachter & Singer, 1962) was designed to test this theory. Physiologically aroused persons who were uninformed or who were misinformed about the various physiological effects of adrenaline injections were more verbally hostile in the presence of an angry companion, or were more euphoric in the presence of a happy companion, than were persons cognisant of the physiological effects of the drug. These labelling effects were consistent with the experimental context.

Other studies have shown similar contextual and labelling effects. Inducing subjects to label arousal produced by means other than frustration as anger, mediates an increase in aggression (Zillmann, 1979) and showing subjects bogus physiological evidence indicating that they are angry increases their level of aggression (Berkowitz & LePage, 1967). Several studies have reported findings consistent with Schachter and Singer's initial results (Ross et al., 1969). Thus, frustrated subjects who are induced to attribute their arousal to sources other than the frustration do not become as aggressive as subjects who are not so induced (Baron & Bell, 1975; Geen, Rakosky, & Pigg, 1972; Harris & Huang, 1974; Nisbett & Schachter, 1966).

The cognitive labelling perspective has also been challenged by some results. Marshall and Zimbardo (1979) compared the emotional states of subjects who received an injection of either placebo or adrenaline. Both groups were misinformed about possible bodily effects from the injections and then exposed to an euphoric confederate. Reports of affect did not differ according to the information provided about their injections. Their inadequately explained psychological arousal did not make them more susceptible to changes in affect. Maslach (1979) employed amnesia for hypnotically induced arousal. Subjects either did or did not experience unexplained arousal in the presence of a confederate who exhibited either happy or angry emotions. The results indicated that subjects with unexplained arousal reported negative emotions regardless of the confederate's mood. The intensity of the arousal and mood manipulation may therefore be important variables.

The two-factor theory of emotion has been extended by one research programme to conditions different from those of Schachter and Singer (1962). Zillmann (1978) proposed an "excitation transfer model", according to which residues from an earlier arousal state intensify a subsequent arousal state. Investigating this proposition, Zillmann, Hoyt, and Day (1974) demonstrated that when provoked subjects could attribute their arousal to immediately preceding strenuous physical exertion, they administered less shock to their provokers than when a delay was interposed that presumably reduced the cues linking their arousal to exertion and led them to mislabel it as anger provoked by the behaviour of a confederate. Bryant and Zillmann (1979) showed that misattribution is more likely when the source of the extraneous arousal is ambiguous. Any activity that increases arousal can, when combined with sufficient provocation, serve as an antecedent of aggression. Because of the anger-labelling that follows excitation transfer, an arousing condition may lead to aggression far beyond the time at which the arousal itself has dissipated. Thus, the misattribution process has implications for long-term behaviour. The labelling of an emotional state may initiate scripted sequences of behaviour: Deciding that one is angry then predisposes one to play out an aggressive script (cf. Abelson, 1981; Schank & Abelson, 1977).

Certain competing positive emotions, e.g. happiness, may actually decrease anger. Bandura (1973) argues that behaviours energised by joyful or euphoric experiences and consistent with happiness do not provoke aggression, even in angry people. Baron and Ball (1974) reported that in subjects who had been provoked to anger by another person, exposure to humorous (nonhostile) cartoons led to significantly less retaliatory aggression than in similarly provoked subjects not shown cartoons. Baron (1978) also found that humour related to sex served to render provoked subjects less aggressive than they would otherwise have been. Thus, excitation transfer may be less likely when arousal is elicited by stimuli that evoke responses that are so different from aggression that they interfere with aggression.

Research using self-reports of anger has consistently found a positive relationship between anger and aggression (Baron, 1972; Gentry, 1970; Rule & Hewitt, 1971). In addition, Megargee, Cook, and Mendelsohn (1967) have found that people who report that they control their anger tend to be less aggressive across a variety of situations than those who do not. It is generally recognised that insult and attack are more powerful and more reliable instigators of aggression than frustration (see Chapter 3). Attack increases emotional reactivity as reflected by increases in heart rate (Ferguson, Rule, & Lindsay, 1982), basal skin conductance (Shortell, Epstein, & Taylor, 1970; Taylor, 1967), and blood pressure (Ax, 1953; Funkenstein, King, & Drolette, 1954). Ferguson et al. (1982) conclude that such conditions promote an increase in anger and that this is revealed in enhanced emotional reactivity and in accompanying verbal reports of anger. However, research that has employed physiological measures of anger has not supplied consistent support for this relationship. Fehr and Stern (1970) argue that it is extremely difficult to distinguish physiologically between emotional states. As a consequence, the relationship between physiologically based measures of anger or aggression may be confounded by other types of physiological arousal, such as fear. Although anger apparently mediates hostile aggression, it may not be a sufficient condition for this response. The link between anger and aggression seems not to be invariant. A variety of other factors influence the relationship. Thus, the circumstances under which increased arousal and anger lead to aggression are determined not only by the prevailing environmental circumstances but also by prior experience and learning.

Attribution is an important cognitive process affecting aggression. The determination, for instance, of how much an action frustrates an individual depends on how the individual perceives the action (e.g. Pastore, 1952). Thus aggression is greater when the subject perceives an act as intentional rather than as accidental (Greenwell & Dengerink, 1973; Nickel, 1974). For example, subjects prevented from performing a task by a confederate who was supposed to have hearing problems were much less aggressive than a similar group who had their task intentionally impeded by a confederate with normal hearing (Burnstein & Worchel, 1962). Judgement of intentionality seems also to be related to the characteristics of the person doing harm. If a person is known to have done a lot of harm in the past, any harmful act by that person will have a strong likelihood of being judged intentional (Ferguson & Rule, 1980). Therefore, stereotypes based on membership of categories such as race, sex, and physical attractiveness also enter into judgements of intent behind harming (Duncan, 1976). The judgement of intentionality will be more likely to result in retaliation when the victim decides that the intent was malicious (Rule, 1978). On the other hand, when frustration is attributed to external factors it provokes less aggression than when it is perceived to be more under the personal control of the subjects (cf. Kulik & Brown, 1979). Zillmann and Cantor (1976) suggest that one reason why attributing the harmful acts of another person to external factors may inhibit aggression is because this type of attribution inhibits anger. People differ both in how easily they are provoked to anger and in their attributions of hostile intent, and these will be discussed under individual differences.

INDIVIDUAL DIFFERENCES AND AGGRESSIVENESS

Defining and measuring individual differences in aggressiveness, as a trait, has not always been deemed successful (cf. Edmunds & Kendrick, 1980; Megargee, 1985). Some extreme views even dismiss the whole notion of personality's relevance to the analysis of behaviour (e.g. Krasner & Ullmann, 1973; Mischel, 1968). Campbell, Bibel, and Muncer (1985) argued that aggressiveness did not have consistency across situations, but some experimental work has refuted this. Deluty (1985) found aggressiveness consistent across times and situations in a range of naturally occurring activities in boys aged between 8 and 10, but not among girls. In addition, Olweus (1979), after reviewing a large number of longitudinal studies with children, found evidence for stability in aggressive behaviour. His findings indicated that general aggressiveness among children is a good predictor of aggressive behaviour. He argues that aggressive behaviour among children "is often maintained irrespective of considerable environmental variation and in opposition to forces acting to change this same behaviour". Evidence to support this comes from a study showing that the higher the levels of aggression reported by children at one point in time, the higher their levels of aggression five years later (Botha & Mels, 1990). Olweus (1979) draws attention to emotional reactions to and cognitive appraisal of the situations as well as other tendencies that may inhibit aggressive responses. In line with this, stability in aggressiveness among children has been explained in terms of cognitive representations of their environment or "schemata" (Huesmann & Eron, 1984). These representations encoded in memory are maintained through rehearsal and can become self-perpetuating, emerging whenever conflict arises. It might be that, when interpersonal conflict occurs, there is an increased likelihood of retrieving violent "scenarios" already rehearsed for that particular occasion. Some of the disagreement concerning the consistency of aggressive behaviour can be resolved by the careful perusal of longitudinal and cross-sectional data. Moffitt (1993) has delineated two distinct categories of adolescents engaging in antisocial behaviour. The larger group only commit such acts during adolescence as a result of the gap emerging between biological and social maturity and imitation of influential antisocal role models or peers. In contrast a small group of individuals exhibit "life-course-persistent" antisocial behaviour, i.e. they engage in such behaviour at every stage of life. Research has taken two directions in this field. First, attempts have been made to identify the characteristics that predispose normal individuals towards aggressive behaviour, and second, the characteristics of people known to be exceptionally violent and accepted as psychologically disturbed have been studied.

Personality traits related to aggression

One aspect of the personality of normal subjects that plays an important role in situations with the potential for aggressive behaviour is impulsivity. Hynan and Grush (1986) found a positive correlation between high levels of impulsivity and aggression toward an experimental partner among male subjects in whom a negative affective state had been induced. If impulse control is an important element for inhibition of aggression, in some cases individuals with chronic overcontrol can behave in an opposite manner. Megargee (1966) argues that these individuals can be characterised by strong defences and inhibitions against aggressing. Thus, when provocation occurs, the associated tension could summate over time until it exceeds the levels of control. Presumably these subjects are habitually passive and thus gain no experience of being mildly aggressive and relieving tension. Belief in one's own ability to control events has also been studied. Subjects who believe they can readily influence events have been named "internals" in contrast to "externals" who feel powerless (Feshbach, 1970). Internals are more likely to engage in aggressive behaviour than externals, although both may exhibit it under extreme provocation.

Two other important differences among individuals in relation to aggressiveness are irritability and emotional susceptibility. Caprara et al. (1985) define the latter characteristic as "the tendency ... to experience feelings of discomfort, helplessness, inadequacy, and vulnerability". High scores on this variable were found in aggressive subjects in comparison with controls (Caprara, Renzi, Alcini, D'Imperio, & Travaglia, 1983). The variable, however, does not interact with provocation in the same way as does irritability. Emotional susceptibility may reflect a more generalised tendency to experience negative affect, which *per se* can be an antecedent of aggression (Berkowitz, 1989). On the other hand, it has been suggested that irritability is a more direct moderator of aggression, leading subjects to react offensively to minimal provocation (Caprara et al., 1983). Older studies suggested that anxiety inhibited the expression of aggression. However, research discriminating different kinds of anxiety has found that this only relates to social inhibition (Taylor, 1970). Fear of social disapproval may prevent the expression of aggressive behaviour except under extreme circumstances.

The personality characteristic of hostility has received a lot of attention from health behaviour research into coronary-prone or Type A behaviour patterns. Briefly, people with this behaviour pattern exhibit three major characteristics. They are competitive, impatient, and hostile (Rosenman & Friedman, 1974). There is a growing body of research showing that people with this behaviour pattern are also more aggressive. They are more likely to exhibit hostile aggression in response to provocation (Carver & Glass, 1978) and to report more interpersonal conflict at work (Baron, 1989). Recently this "hostility syndrome" has been linked to brain serotonin systems (Williams, 1994) (see Chapter 2).

Finally, there has been some recent interest in shame-proneness. This has been distinguished from guilt as it involves negative evaluations of the self (Tangney, 1990). People who report more shame-proneness on questionnaires also report more anger and aggression (Tangney, Wagner, Fletcher, & Gramzow, 1992).

Thus, many different personality characteristics are important in the occurrence of aggression. Social learning theorists would claim that situational factors are much more important but evidence is accruing that personality may influence the learning of behaviour and shaping of overt responses (Clarke & Hoyle, 1988): People may interpret situational factors in different ways. Thus, Dodge (1993) has identified different types of processing styles in children. Severely aggressive boys are not only more likely to interpret ambiguous or accidental acts as having hostile intentions, they are also more likely to demonstrate actual errors in the interpretation of interpersonal behaviour when the cues are clear (Dodge et al., 1984). This "hostile attributional bias" is correlated with undersocialised, interpersonal, aggressive behaviour (reactive aggression) but not with nonviolent crime or socialised delinquency (Dodge, Price, Bachorowski, & Newman, 1990a).

Pathological aggression
A small proportion of people are responsible for a very large number of extremely aggressive acts and so the study of their characteristics may help us to elucidate the components of aggression. Although the term "aggression" is not specifically defined in the fourth edition of the American Psychiatry Association's Diagnostic and Statistical Manual of Mental Disorders (APA, 1994), it overlaps with certain subtypes of personality disorder and other abnormal mental conditions, e.g borderline and antisocial personality disorder. Tyrer (1988) defines personality disorder as "a persistent abnormality of personal and social functioning that is independent of mental integration". In this connection several subtypes of personality disorder are associated with aggressive behaviour in varying degrees. Violence among these patients is a stable characteristic present from an early age (Benezech, Bourgeois, & Yesavage, 1980; Kermani, 1981), not associated with

emotional turmoil or any specific symptom cluster (Craig, 1982; Kermani, 1981), and resistant to change (Kermani, 1981). The history of violence usually starts before or around puberty; when it appears later it is much more likely to be due to an identifiable brain disease or psychosis (Kermani, 1981). As personality disorders in general form a heterogeneous group without clear-cut neurological or psychiatric disorder, efforts to define a specific personality disorder for aggressive patients have failed (cf. Kermani, 1981) and there has been much discussion on the use of traits rather than behaviour or categories (Stone, 1993; Widiger, 1992). However, some consistency is seen in the history of such individuals. Perinatal difficulties may play a role in predisposing individuals to aggression but only when combined with an unstable family environment (Mednick, Brennan, & Kandel, 1988). Not infrequently a history is found of parental discord, often with divorce, separation, or death, as well as parental alcoholism, (Bach-Y-Rita & Veno, 1974; Faretra, 1981). Physical abuse in childhood seems to be a major risk (Dodge, Bates, & Pettit, 1990b) and has been found to be more predictive of aggressive behaviour in young adult men than paternal alcoholism (Pollock et al., 1990). Moreover, a deficient rearing environment is much more commonly found for violent individuals with a diagnosis of personality disorder than in those with a diagnosis of psychosis (Benezech et al., 1980; Kermani, 1981). Other characterological difficulties such as poor self-image (Kermani, 1981) and depressive traits may be present (Bach-Y-Rita, 1974).

The antisocial, "psychopathic", or "sociopathic" personality is the one most frequently linked to aggression. Monahan (1981), however, has noted that in studies of violence these diagnoses are often ill-defined and may not be independent of the history of criminal behaviour. He averred that the essential feature of this disorder is a continuous history of behaviour that violates the rights of others. Aggression would be one element of a pattern of lying, stealing, truancy, fighting, substance abuse, and disrespect for authority manifest through childhood and adolescence. The more flagrant antisocial behaviour diminishes during adult life, although the deficits in interpersonal relationship skills are sustained. Such persons often perceive others as being hostile toward them. Millon (1981) has criticised the term "antisocial personality disorder", pointing out that a type of behaviour cannot be used to define a disorder of personality. He preferred the term "aggressive personality", defined by traits of hostile affectivity, social rebelliousness, vindictiveness, and disregard for danger. Blackburn (1993) has argued that psychopaths may be construed as individuals showing a more extreme coercive style, but people displaying pathological aggression are not a homogeneous group.

Two investigators have published representative studies describing extremely aggressive individuals (Megargee, 1966; Toch, 1980). Toch (1980) arranged long interviews with 77 prisoners and recent parolees in penal institutions. He described three main types of aggressive personality. The "self-indulgent compensator", the most common type, were those individuals with both a very low self-opinion and a fear that others would come to share this view. In order to protect these susceptibilities, they responded aggressively to even the slightest insult or provocation. The "self-indulger" represented those individuals who clung to the infantile view that others exist simply to satisfy their needs and wants. Violence would emerge when people did not pander to their whims. A third group, the "self-defender", was made up of those who displayed an intense fear of others attacking them and therefore attacked pre-emptively.

Individuals who exhibit chronic violence or whose violence is momentary but exceedingly brutal have also been studied by Megargee (1966). Following extensive interviews, he delineated two types of violent individuals. The first type he called "undercontrolled", individuals with a lack of control or inhibitions that normally prevent people from engaging in aggression. The second type, whom he called "overcontrolled", included men who normally inhibit aggression but commit extremely violent acts when their frustration is no longer containable. Undercontrolled offenders may have a history of many moderate acts of aggression, but overcontrolled offenders usually have been convicted of single acts of extreme violence. These people possess strong inhibitions against displaying aggression and therefore show extreme restraint in the face of repeated provocations. However, the latter mount up until the inhibitions are finally overcome and they erupt into sudden violence. These contrasting personality types have been investigated in the field of domestic violence (Subotnik, 1989). It was found that men who battered their wives could have either personality. Those classified as undercontrolled had a history of violence towards others, approved of aggression, experienced little guilt but felt impulsive and powerless. In contrast, those classified as overcontrolled had not been violent to others, disapproved of aggression, and were low in impulsivity. They indicated that the incidents had occurred after they had abused alcohol and they felt very guilty.

Blackburn (1971) investigated Megargee's hypothesis and found four instead of two groups among mentally disordered offenders. To investigate these further, he constructed a questionnaire (Special Hospitals Assessment of Personality and Socialisation (SHAPS); Blackburn, 1982). Cluster analysis on the results of the SHAPS has consistently reproduced four categories of personality deviation in the special hospitals population (Blackburn, 1986): primary psychopaths (impulsive, aggressive, hostile, extraverted, self-confident, low to average anxiety); secondary psychopaths (hostile, impulsive, aggressive, socially anxious, withdrawn, moody, low self-esteem); controlled (defensive, controlled, sociable, very low anxiety); and inhibited (shy, withdrawn, controlled, moderately anxious, low self-esteem). Blackburn and associates (Blackburn, 1993) then went on to look at the social expectations of these groups. They isolated three factors: others could be viewed as challenging, attentive, or yielding, and the groups differed in their expectations. Primary psychopaths do not expect others to be challenging but they expect them to be both attentive and yielding, whereas secondary psychopaths expect them to be challenging but not attentive or yielding. The controlled and inhibited groups did not expect challenge or attention.

Clinical features

In contrast to media accounts, the vast majority of those with severe psychiatric disorders are not violent or dangerous. However, a small subgroup may be violent both in hospital and in the community (Torrey, 1994). Violent behaviour should be understood in relation to other clinical features present in the underlying disorder. Thus, the severity of psychopathology appears to correlate with frequency of violent acts in psychiatric patients. Violent in-patients were more impaired than nonviolent ones with regard to delusions, hallucinations, inappropriate affect, and bizarre behaviour (Tardiff & Sweillam, 1980). Another study of violent schizophrenics reported that aggression was accompanied by delusions and hallucinations, and typified by unprovoked destruction of property and self-injury in addition to explosive, murderous onslaughts. These attacks were accompanied by retrograde amnesia, leaving the patients perplexed by their actions (Plananski & Johnston, 1977). Similarly, Noble and Rodger (1989) compared in-patients who committed violent assaults with matched controls during one year in the Bethlem Royal and Maudsley Hospital. A significantly higher proportion of patients with delusions and hallucinations and an increased incidence of schizophrenia was found among the patients with assaultive behaviour, confirming the results of previous similar studies (Fottrell, 1980; Pearson, Wilmot, & Podi, 1986; Tardiff, 1981). Violence has also been reported in association with paranoid delusions or ideation, whether in paranoid schizophrenia, paranoia, or paraphrenia. Benezech et al. (1980) conducted a study in a French hospital for the criminally insane and found the largest number of murderers was among the patients with paranoid delusions. Most of the violence of these patients was directed at a specific person, usually a significant individual in the patient's life. The same researchers studied patients in several other French psychiatric institutions (Addad, Benezech, Bourgeois, & Yesavage, 1981), contrasting the crimes committed by paranoid schizophrenics with those carried out by chronic undifferentiated schizophrenics. Violence occurring in the context of more disorganised psychotic behaviour (undifferentiated schizophrenics) was less focused, less planned, and often less dangerous.

The relation between violence and depression has been commented on in the literature, although the incidence of actual violence in major depression is rare. The expression of depression in violent patients varies from transient dysphoria accompanying the violent outburst to chronic depressive traits (Bach-Y-Rita, 1974; Bach-Y-Rita & Veno, 1974; Faretra, 1981; Planansky & Johnston, 1977; Tardiff & Sweillam, 1982). These chronic depressive traits are prominent in certain categories of violent patients with personality disorder and appear to be part of their characterological makeup (Bach-Y-Rita, 1974; Bach-Y-Rita & Veno, 1974; Kermani, 1981). A common biological mechanism has been advanced in the literature with regard to the role of the neurotransmitter serotonin (5-HT) and its putative dysfunction in aggressive behaviour (see Chapter 2). Impulsivity and depressed mood are also associated with 5-HT imbalance, and anxiety disorders have been linked to the same biochemical substrate (cf. van Praag et al., 1987). More practically, clinical data support the view that depressed mood, anxiety, and aggression are closely related (Apter et al., 1990; Kahn, van Praag, Wetzler, Asnis, & Barr, 1988; Kotler et al., 1993), e.g. a subtype of depressed patients show not only increased suicidality but also have high hostility and aggression ratings (Farmer, 1987) and may exhibit anger attacks (Fava, Anderson, & Rosenbaum, 1990).

Genetic factors

Genetic influences on aggression in lower animals are well recognised. Lagerspetz (1979) bred mice selectively for aggressiveness, with inherited aggressive tendencies emerging as early as the second generation. The biological basis and the phytogenetic history of antagonistic behaviours seems unquestionable (cf. Fromm, 1973). However, degrees of freedom of the organism are also inherent in its encoded genotype, only a portion of which can come to potential expression, partly as a result of internal and external environmental events. This constitutes the effective genotype, which interacts further with developmental events to determine the final phenotype (Lindzey, Loehlin, Manosevitz, & Thiessen, 1971; Vale & Vale, 1969). Fisher (1955, cited in Selmanoff & Ginsburg, 1981), for example, found that particular pedigrees of terriers had the potential for extreme aggression, depending on conditions of early rearing.

Has similar evidence been found for human beings? One initial difficulty is methodological in nature. Human reproduction cannot be controlled through selective breeding in the same way as that of lower animals. Consequently, twin studies have been the main tool in human genetic research.

Rushton, Fulker, Neale, Nias, and Eysenck (1986) presented evidence that aggressiveness is partially hereditary in humans. Five personality variables (altruism, empathy, nurturance, assertiveness, and aggressiveness) were measured in 573 pairs of monozygotic and dizygotic twins. The monozygotic group had higher correlations in each personality variable. In studies of twins reared apart, impulsivity as a personality trait has been shown to be partly heritable in both healthy (Coccaro & Bergeman, 1993) and psychiatric (Torgerson, 1984) populations. Although borderline personality disorder itself does not appear to be inherited (Torgerson, 1984), relatives of patients with this disorder are more likely to display traits of impulsivity and affective instability (Silverman et al., 1991). These studies indicate that positive and negative personality traits related to aggression may be genetically connected.

Another area of genetic studies of human aggression concerns the XYY karyotype. Although the first discovery of a man with an extra chromosome (Sandberg, Koeph, Ishinara, & Hauschka, 1961) found that he was not especially aggressive or criminal, extensive research was then undertaken in an attempt to establish links between genes, criminality, and violence. Price and Whatmore (1967) showed that aggressive behaviour that was related to an extra Y chromosome was present even among males raised in family environments of no more than average aggressiveness. Moreover, the ratio of XYY males to normals in prisons and other security institutions ranges from about 1:35 to 1:100, whereas that in the population at large has been estimated as approximately 1:550 (Court-Brown, 1968). These findings seem to implicate a defect in the nervous system that is genetically determined (Jacobs, Brunton, Melville, Brittain, & McClermont, 1965). The extra Y chromosome has also been connected with higher male sexual hormone levels, which could lead XYY males to be differentiated from average people (Selmanoff & Ginsburg, 1981). This could account for their potential aggressiveness as well as for their unusual height (Daly, 1969).

On the other hand, the correlational nature of the data allows other possible explanations. Schiavi, Theilgaard, Owen, and White (1984) found no association between XYY or XXY chromosomal abnormalities and violence outside correctional institutions. Witkin and his associates (1976) found that the XYY karyotype was related to both criminal behaviour and low intelligence, but not to overall aggressiveness. Heritability of criminality is not the same as heritability of aggressiveness. Bohman, Cloninger, Sigvardsson, and Von Knorring (1982) in a study of adopted men failed to show that their violent crimes were related to violence in their biological or adoptive parents, but rather to other causes, such as alcohol abuse. However, nonviolent petty property crimes do seem to have a genetic predisposition, a finding confirmed by a positive relationship between the conviction rate of adoptees and their biological father but not their adopted father (Mednick, Gabrielli, & Hutchings, 1987). Any association with arrest for crimes is probably linked to other factors, such as low intelligence.

Cognitive correlates

Individual variations in the level of cognitive development also influence aggression in response to both provocation and the observation of violence being carried out by others (cf. Parke & Slaby, 1983). In addition, poor cognitive development may be associated with high levels of delinquency and with a generally negative self-image (Feshbach & Price, 1984; Pitkanen-Pulkinen, 1979). However, these cognitive deficits may be small and therefore are often disregarded. They are not believed to be deterministic but rather part of a complex interaction (Moffitt, 1990). Comparing cognitive function between prisoners remanded for violent crimes and those remanded for nonviolent crimes, Robertson, Taylor, and Gunn (1987) found that although the violent group were of slightly lower general ability, this was not significant. Some research has attempted to link impaired frontal lobe function with antisocial behaviour, but the evidence supports a general relationship with the impaired regulation of complex social behaviour rather than aggression *per se*, and even then is not clear-cut (Kandel & Freed, 1989).

Attitudes and aggression

Attitudes or beliefs may also influence behaviour of all kinds. This is most likely to occur when external influences are minimal, the attitude is specific to the behaviour, and we are conscious or made aware of our attitudes (Myers, 1994). Attitudes about aggressive behaviour are likely to influence its expression in many differing ways. Most research in this area, however, has focused on prejudice, i.e. negative attitudes toward members of a particular social group. It has generally been found that highly prejudiced people tend to be more aggressive than less prejudiced ones regardless of the target. It has therefore been suggested that both prejudice and aggression may be products of "a hostile disposition".

Gender differences in aggression

Gender is another variable that has been implicated in aggression, although the underlying cause is disputed. Maccoby and Jacklin (1974, 1980) argue that in most societies men are generally more aggressive than women. They contend that male–female differences in aggression begin too early in life to be attributed confidently to learning and that a hormonal basis for sex differences in humans as well as other species may play a crucial role (see p.36). This evidence has been criticised by other investigators, who argue that the case for a genetic basis for sex differences in aggression has not been properly established (Tieger, 1980). Hyde (1984) reviewed 143 studies on sex differences in aggression, including those studies previously reviewed by Maccoby and Jacklin (1980), which involved subjects ranging in age from 2.5 to 35 years, and found smaller sex differences related to aggression. Moreover, aggression diminished with age. Eagly and Steffen (1986) in another review, with adult subjects, corroborated Hyde's findings. However, some of those who propose a genetic link to sex differences concede that a large part of male–female differences is traceable to social learning (cf. Frodi, Macaulay, & Thome, 1977). The idea that men prefer physical aggression and women favour verbal means of aggression (Bandura, 1973; Buss, 1963) is weakly supported, and women are more likely than men to experience guilt and anxiety over aggressing (e.g. Brock & Buss, 1964; Wyer, Weatherly, & Terrell, 1965). Other sex differences occur at a more cognitive level. Men and women have somewhat different ways of interpreting provoking situations and may differ in aggression as a result (cf. Duncan & Hobson, 1977; Frodi et al., 1977). The two sexes also tend to react to observed violence in contrasting ways, and this can be attributed to different values placed on aggression as a way of reacting to conflict (Cantor, Zillman, & Einsiedel, 1978).

SUMMARY

In this chapter we discussed definitions of aggression and concluded that intention to harm is an important element whether this is motivated primarily by affect or by some other goal. Historically, theories of aggression have developed from instinct and drive to broader approaches incorporating emotions and cognitions and recognising the importance of learned methods of responding. Several factors increase the likelihood of aggressive behaviour and these can be divided into three broad categories: interpersonal, external, and individual differences. Aggression occurs within an interpersonal exchange and thus much research has been devoted to elements such as frustration, provocation, attack, and instigation from others. Attack is the most reliable way of inducing aggression, but even so the response can be modified by perceived intentionality or apology. Adverse environmental factors may also increase the likelihood of aggression. This may be linked to increased arousal or negative affect. Other external factors such as pain, substance abuse, and the mass media have effects on aggression. Watching violence on television is associated with aggression in children. It is likely that this effect is mediated through social learning and that children with a hostile disposition or in an adverse family environment are most at risk. Individual differences in aggressiveness are important and may be partially hereditary. Various personality characteristics seem to be important in the normal population but a small proportion of people are responsible for a very large number of extreme aggressive acts. The most prevalent diagnosis among these individuals is personality disorder. The pattern of aggressive behaviour starts early in life and may be associated with both perinatal difficulties and an unstable family environment. These individuals may also show a hostile attributional bias, i.e. they expect provocation from others and therefore perceive it in neutral situations.

CHAPTER TWO

The psychopharmacology of aggression

In this chapter, we review some of the aspects of the psychopharmacology of aggression. Anatomical topics are introduced first as they are relevant to the biochemical actions of various drugs on aggression. The importance of 5-HT is apparent and a review is presented of the effects of serotonergic drugs on aggression. An outline is also given of the clinical actions of various psychotropic drugs on aggression.

BRAIN MECHANISMS

One of the major attempts to understand the role of brain mechanisms in the regulation of aggressive behaviour was made by Moyer (1976). He suggested that in both humans and lower animals, functionally different structures in the CNS were related to different types of aggression. Thus, Moyer (1976) suggested a scheme to explain aggression that would involve: (1) a number of innate systems of neural organisation in the brain, with one such pattern for each kind of aggression; (2) activation of the innate systems by appropriate stimuli; and (3) a system for the generation of arousal (the reticular activating system) that affects both the organism's reactivity to the aforesaid stimuli and the intensity of the aggression induced by the innate neural system. This innate system would also be sensitive to other systems in the body, and would be linked to specific patterns of motor behaviour by which the aggression is acted out (Moyer, 1976).

This classification has been criticised by Herbert (1993) as confounding stimuli, contexts, and functions. In applying reductionism to the experimental study of any behaviour, we risk neglecting important contextual cues, but this may be more important with aggression as Herbert (1993) claims that it usually occurs as part of another behaviour. Aggressive behaviour is not a goal in itself but is used as a means to an end. Aggressive behaviour is fairly stereotyped and species-specific, which indicates that it must be organised by a neural system, but in trying to seek this system it is important to recognise the other behaviour of which aggression is a part. As aggression is an optional component, the mechanism involved may determine whether it is appropriate in the circumstances. Herbert (1993) entitles this "a tactical decision".

Efforts have been made to fit specific areas of the brain to the expression of aggressive behaviour. Various parts of the limbic system have been implicated, in particular the amygdala. Both the temporal lobe cortex and the medial limbic structures such as the hypothalamus are linked to the amygdala. Lesions of the amygdala in both primates and humans produce calming or "taming" effects. Conversely, electrical stimulation of the amygdala or hypothalamus can precipitate aggressive responses.

Data related to the involvement of the amygdala in aggression in humans come from reports dealing with surgical intervention aimed at the relief of organic brain disease not responsive to other clinical treatment. Control of violent and homicidal outbursts in previously intractable psychiatric patients after amygdalectomy was claimed in many studies in the 1960s and 1970s. However, a review of these studies (O'Callaghan & Carroll, 1982) shows many to be flawed and the overall results for amygdalectomy to be unimpressive. There are grave doubts about the specificity of operative effects. Surgery often results in a general change and any positive effects on aggressive behaviour may occur in the context of a general dampening of function.

Nevertheless, animal work has continued to link the amygdala to aggressive behaviour. Neurotoxin-induced lesions in the basolateral nuclei have been shown to reduce aggressive behaviour in the rat (McGregor & Herbert, 1992). The amygdala has been represented as linking cognitive and limbic function, thus allowing affective value to be assigned to stimuli. LeDoux (1989) suggests that there may be various pathways leading to different levels of processing. The projections from the thalamus would be involved in processing the affective significance of simple sensory cues, whereas those from the cortex would be involved in the processing of more complex stimuli. These would be allied to Lazarus' primary and secondary appraisal patterns (Lazarus, 1991), i.e. first is there a threat?, and second, how can I cope? It has been suggested that the amygdala contains the neural representation of fear. If amygdaloid lesions reduce fear and therefore threat, then the likelihood of an aggressive response may be reduced. The amygdala may then be involved in "tactical decisions" on the use of or response to aggressive behaviour (Herbert, 1993).

Animal work has also linked the temporal lobe to aggression. In rats, increased aggression is seen with experimentally induced foci in temporal lobe structures (Pinel, Treit, & Rovner, 1977). In humans the association of the temporal lobe and aggression has come from studies of patients suffering from epilepsy (Devinsky & Bear, 1984; Mark & Ervin, 1970; St. Hilaire, Gilbert, Bouvier, & Barbeau, 1980). Violent aggressive behaviour reported concomitant to seizures is usually stereotyped, unsustained, and not purposeful in nature (Delgado-Escueta, Mattson, & King, 1981). Ictal aggression is rare. However, it depends on the thought content of the patient at the time and is thus much more likely to be a problem in the community than when being carefully recorded in hospital (Fenwick, 1986).

It has been suggested that the relationship between aggression and epilepsy is a consequence of temporary disconnection between medial limbic structures and cortical centres of control (Ferguson, Rayport, & Corrie, 1986), which could disrupt appraisal systems. Moreover, aggressive outbursts in patients suffering from temporal lobe epilepsy have been viewed as a trait-like behaviour, which usually appears in the nonictal phase (Ramani & Gumnit, 1981). This might reflect decreased perfusion and metabolism in the area of the epileptic foci (Valmier, Touchon, Daures, Zanca, & Baldy-Moulinier, 1987). Based on the asymmetry of the human brain, a comparison of patients with unilateral right or left anterior temporal spiking foci has indicated that the right focus is associated with elation and optimism, and the left focus facilitates humourlessness, sadness, obsessiveness, anger, and aggressiveness (Bear & Fedio, 1977; Mandell, 1978).

Episodic dyscontrol has been suggested to be a consequence of neurophysiological dysfunction of the limbic system (limbic ictus) (Monroe, 1970). Monroe (1982) argues that although an EEG abnormality is usually not found, support for his theory of limbic ictal phenomena rests with the response of individuals with the dyscontrol syndrome to anticonvulsant treatments. However, Leicester (1982) examined 500 cases referred to a neurologist and found that of the 17 patients referred for temper tantrums, none had organic factors (epilepsy or episodic dyscontrol syndrome). Rather, the violent episodes were the result of psychological factors. Furthermore, Hermann and Whitman (1984) reviewed 64 studies conducted in the previous 20 years that assessed the relation between temporal lobe epilepsy, aggression, and other forms of psychopathology. They focused on studies of the interictal period in terms of irritable, aggressive, or hostile behaviour using neurosurgical and non-neurosurgical patients, as well as surveys of prison populations. They concluded that controlled investigations showed no overall differences in the levels of violence between persons with and without epilepsy. Any association between aggression and epilepsy is likely to be due to nonspecific factors, including associated brain damage (Treiman, 1991).

Most of the classic neuroanatomical studies are conducted in lower animals, but as they also intervene in the normal functioning of the CNS, i.e. they are invasive, we must be cautious in interpreting and generalising the results to humans. New techniques using noninvasive images of the brain, such as positron emission tomography (PET), single photon emission tomography (SPET), or magnetic resonance imaging (MRI), are likely to provide us with much more information in the future. Thus, brain abnormalities not detected by conventional EEG technology can already be picked up by brain imaging. To date the number of violent individuals studied has been small but damage has been shown in the predicted areas, i.e. the amygdala, the temporal lobe and left hemisphere dysfunction seems to be more common.

NEUROCHEMICAL ASPECTS

Neurochemical systems in the body may sensitise the organism to various conditions for aggression and make such behaviour more likely. Attempts have been made to link modifications in various neurotransmitter systems with changes in various types of aggressive behaviour. Research has focused on five CNS neurotransmitter systems, i.e. 5-hydroxytryptamine (5-HT), gamma-amino butyric acid (GABA) and dopamine (DA) that are largely inhibitory, and noradrenaline (NA), largely excitatory, as well as acetylcholine (ACh).

Behavioural paradigms to measure aggression in animals grew out of experimental psychology and ethology (see Table 2.1). Exposure to aversive living conditions, such as deprivation of social contact or crowding, or the administration of aversive stimuli, such as shocks, are used to induce aggressive behaviour in habitually nonaggressive animals. Alternatively, predatory behaviour, such as mouse-killing by rats, is studied. Reis (1974) has suggested two major categories of animal aggression: predatory, such as the mouse-killing behaviour of

TABLE 2.1
Paradigms used to study behavioural aggression in animals

Experimental psychology	Ethology
Isolation-induced	Predatory
Pain-elicited	Social dominance
Extinction-induced	Resident-intruder
	Maternal

rats, and affective, such as isolation-induced fighting in mice, intruder aggression, and pain-induced or shock-induced fighting in rodents. These standard laboratory paradigms have been used to study the activity of the different neurotransmitter systems on aggressive behaviour.

Aggressive behaviour appears to be enhanced by activation of the cholinergic system (Grossman, 1963). Aggressive behaviour can be produced by an injection of carbachol, a cholinomimetic drug, into the amygdala of cats. If the same drug is injected into the lateral hypothalamus of rats, predatory aggression will be increased. The behaviour is suppressed when methylatropine is applied centrally (Smith, King, & Hoebel, 1970). Also the injection of physostigmine, a cholinesterase inhibitor, into the amygdala of rats increased aggressive behaviour during a shock-induced fighting paradigm (Rodgers & Brown, 1976). In the same paradigm, aggression was abolished by cholinergic blockade (Powell, Milligan, & Walters, 1973). In humans, enhanced cholinergic receptor sensitivity has been linked to affective disorders (Janowsky & Risch, 1987), but may be associated with more general negative mood or dysphoria. In normal males, dysphoric responses to physostigmine have been shown to correlate with traits of irritability and emotional lability (Fritze et al., 1990), and in personality-disordered patients, dysphoric responses are most prominent in those with affective instability (Coccaro & Siever, 1995).

Central dopamine also appears to stimulate fighting in laboratory animals. Drugs that increase dopamine levels in the brain, like levodopa and apomorphine, a dopamine agonist, have been found to produce aggressive behaviour in rodents and defensive "boxing" behaviour in rats, respectively (Lammers & van Rossum, 1968). Dopamine antagonists are effective in reversing aggression (Yen, Stangler, & Millman, 1959) in shock-induced fighting in rats previously treated with an infusion of dopamine into the cerebral ventricles (Geyer & Segal, 1974).

The involvement of the GABA-ergic system in aggression has also been studied. Puglisi-Allegra and Mandel (1980) found that activation of central GABA activity decreases isolation-induced fighting in mice and shock-induced fighting in rats (Puglisi-Allegra, Simler, & Kempf, 1981). Thus, enhanced GABA activity inhibits aggression. Conversely, decreasing GABA activity may increase aggressive behaviour. Central GABA activity is augmented through activation of benzodiazepine receptors and so treatment with benzodiazepines would be expected to reduce aggressive behaviour. In line with this, benzodiazepine treatment has been associated with successfully controlling aggressive behaviour in brain-lesioned rats (Randall, Schaller, & Heise, 1960) and shock-induced fighting in rodents (Christmas & Maxwell, 1970). In contrast with these data, benzodiazepines have also been shown to increase aggressive behaviour under various conditions (Mos & Olivier, 1987). Benzodiazepine-induced aggression seems to differ according to species and compound tested (Krsiak & Sulcova, 1990). It is not clear if pro-aggressive effects are exclusively benzodiazepine receptor-mediated, but the benzodiazepine-$GABA_A$-C1 ionophore complex also seems to be an important site for the effects of alcohol on aggression (Miczek, Weerts, & DeBold, 1993). Alcohol-mediated aggression can be potentiated by benzodiazepine agonists and reversed by antagonists. Work in humans will be discussed later under benzodiazepines and in Chapters 6 and 7.

Noradrenaline has different effects on aggressive behaviour depending on the paradigm used. The enhanced central level of NA produced by tricyclic antidepressants exerts an inhibitory effect on predatory aggression (mouse-killing behaviour, cf. Katz, 1976). In contrast, most data support a facilitory role in affective or irritable aggression (Stolk, Conner, Levine, & Barchas, 1984). For example, artificially induced stress in rats (depriving them of REM sleep, or immobilisation for several hours a day for a month) produces irritability and shock-induced fighting after several days in association with altered central noradrenergic receptors (Eichelman & Hegstrand, 1982; Lamprecht, Eichelman, & Thoa, 1972). It is argued that this effect is caused by down-regulation of cortical beta-adrenergic receptors and increased activity of the noradrenaline synthesis enzyme tyrosine hydroxylase in the brain stem (Eichelman & Hegstrand, 1982) and hypothalamus (Lamprecht et al., 1972). On the other hand, intraventricular infusion of noradrenaline into normal rats reduces shock-induced fighting (Geyer & Segal, 1974). Further, depletion of central noradrenaline with the neurotoxin 6-hydroxydopa enhances shock-induced fighting in the rat (Thoa, Eichelman, & Richardson, 1972). Considering that this effect takes several days to develop fully, it has been attributed to a supersensitivity to endogenous noradrenaline. Human work has confirmed the association between enhanced noradrenergic activity and increased irritability. A positive correlation has been found between irritability, impulsivity, and CSF concentrations of 4,5-methyl-hydroxyphenylglycol (MHPG), a major metabolite of noradrenaline (Roy, De Jong, & Linnoila, 1989). Also, an augmented growth hormone response to clonidine has been shown to correlate with subscales of the Buss Durkee Hostility Inventory (Coccaro et al., 1991; Trestman et al., 1992). It has thus been suggested that the noradrenergic system plays a major role in responsiveness to the environment and reactivity to threatening stimuli.

Among all the neurotransmitter systems involved in aggressive behaviour, convergence of animal and human research is best exemplified by the serotonergic system. 5-HT receptors are now known to constitute a complex series of subtypes, e.g. 5-HT_1, 5-HT_2, and even sub-subtypes, e.g. 5-HT_{1A} (Harrington, Zhong, Garlow, & Ciaranello, 1992). At least 15 receptor types are now proposed based on evidence of cloning but the number increases rapidly. Attention has focused on 5-HT_{1A}, 5-HT_2, and 5-HT_3 receptors and various agonists and antagonists are being evaluated in a wide range of psychiatric disorders including aggression. However, the physiological specificity of these receptors is still being clarified. Lowering central serotonin levels enhances both affective and predatory aggression in laboratory animals (Eichelman, 1988). One important role of a normally functioning serotonin system is to facilitate appropriate delays in behavioural responses to various environmental stimuli (Sanger & Blackman, 1976), as well as the release of inhibition of "punished behaviours" (Tye, Everitt, & Iversen, 1977; Tye, Iversen, & Green, 1979). An extrapolation of similar behaviour in humans would be the relative incapacity of aggressive individuals to "delay gratification" (cf. Soubrié, 1986). Abnormalities of the serotonergic system in patients with different psychiatric diagnoses correlate with impulsive inward and outward directed aggressive behaviours (Asberg, Schalling, Traskman-Bendz, & Wagner, 1987) but not with premeditated acts of violence (Brown & Linnoila, 1990; Linnoila & Virkkunen, 1992). This suggests that violence itself is not necessarily associated with decreased central 5-HT activity. Coccaro, Kavoussi, and Lesser (1992) have suggested that central 5-HT dysfunction may represent a behavioural trait (irritability), which could be characterised by a "tendency to respond" aggressively to adverse stimuli, rather than the actual act of aggression, and others have suggested that it is impulsivity rather than aggression that is correlatd with decreased central 5-HT activity. Serotonin may in fact be involved in the appraisal process so that abnormalities of the system mean that individuals are both more likely to perceive threat and to attribute blame. Interrelationships have in fact been found between violence risk and suicide risk, anger, impulsivity, and anxiety (Apter et al., 1990).

In humans, evidence supporting an association between serotonergic system dysfunction and aggression comes from five main sources: studies in suicidal populations (e.g. Asberg, Thoren, & Traskman, 1976a); with patients with impulsive aggressive behaviours (e.g. Brown, Goodwin, Ballenger, Goyer & Major, 1979; Brown et al., 1982); 5-HT receptor-related studies (e.g. Coccaro & Astill, 1990); familial and genetic factors related to the 5-HT system (e.g. Linnoila, De Jong, & Vikkunen, 1989); and neuroendocrine challenges with drugs that interfere with 5-HT activity (e.g. Meltzer & Lowe, 1987).

Evidence for a low cerebrospinal fluid (CSF) 5-hydroxyindoleacetic acid (5-HIAA) concentration in patients with depression and with associated vegetative symptoms was first observed by van Praag and Korf (1971). In a subsequent study, Asberg, Traskman, and Thoren (1976b) demonstrated an association between low CSF 5-HIAA concentrations and violent suicide attempts in depressed patients. Subsequently many other CSF studies (e.g. Banki, Arato, Papp, & Kurcz, 1984; Traskman, Asberg, Bertilsson, & Sjostrand, 1981) have confirmed the relation between CSF 5-HIAA and attempts at suicide in patients with unipolar depression, personality disorder, or schizophrenia (Lester, 1995). Furthermore, low brain serotonin turnover, as indicated by low CSF 5-HIAA levels, correlates negatively with scores on the impulsiveness scale of the Karolinska Scale of Personality (Schalling & Asberg, 1984). Consequently, impulsive or violent suicidal behaviour may be considered as the product of inhibiting (mediated by 5-HT) and activating (mediated by other neurotransmitter systems, such as noradrenaline and dopamine) a neuronal system (Depue & Spoont, 1986).

Abnormalities of the serotonin system may have a wider role in relation to aggression and violence. Brown et al. (1979, 1982) found strong negative correlations between 5-HIAA levels and a history of aggressive behaviour, suicide attempts, and scores on the Buss-Durkee Hostility Inventory, and the psychopathic deviate scale from the Minnesota Multiphasic Personality Inventory, in patients with personality disorder. Further analyses of these data suggest that individuals with low CSF 5-HIAA had shown disturbed behaviour during childhood (Brown & Goodwin, 1984). Linnoila et al. (1983) also found a linear association between low CSF 5-HIAA and murder and attempted murder in patients whose crimes were assessed as impulsive, by comparison with nonimpulsive violent offenders who had premeditated their crimes. Moreover, offenders who had committed more than one violent crime had lower levels than those who had committed only one such crime, and impulsive offenders who had attempted suicide had lower levels than violent offenders who had never attempted suicide. In addition, CSF 5-HIAA levels are lower in arsonists than in nonimpulsive violent offenders or normal controls (Virkkunen, Nuutila, Goodwin, & Linnoila, 1987).

Post-mortem brain studies of suicide victims have also revealed pre-synaptic (Asberg et al., 1987) and post-synaptic indices of serotonin turnover to be changed (Arora & Meltzer, 1989). The index of pre-synaptic 5-HT function was the binding of tritiated imipramine to the brain tissue: A reduction of maximal binding of imipramine was found in various brain areas (Crow et al., 1984; Gross-Isseroff, Israeli, & Biegon, 1989; Paul, Rehavi, Skolnik, & Goodwin, 1984; Stanley, Virgilio, & Gershon, 1982), suggesting a possible loss of 5-HT pre-synaptic receptors. However, Owen et al. (1986) and Meyerson et al. (1982) reported respectively no alteration and an increase in the number of pre-synaptic serotonin receptors. In contrast, post-synaptic upregulation of the 5-HT_2 receptors in the frontal cortex has been reported in impulsive aggressive and suicidal individuals (Arora & Meltzer, 1989; Mann, Stanley, McBride, & McEwen, 1986; Stanley & Mann, 1983). In addition, a decrease of function mediated by 5-HT_1 receptors seems to occur (Gudelsky, Koenig, & Meltzer, 1986). This reciprocal effect has received support from behavioural responses to antidepressant treatment (Pericic & Manev, 1988), and animal studies that have indicated that 5-HT_1 receptors, in contrast to 5-HT_2, have an important role in the mediation of behavioural inhibition (McMillen, Scott, William, & Sanghera, 1987). On the other hand, the claim that increased 5-HT_2 activity would be a compensatory mechanism to down-regulation in the pre-synaptic terminals has not received empirical support. Increasing either the number of 5-HT_2 receptors or their responses to chemical stimulation is not followed by pre-synaptic 5-HT depletion (Blackshear, Steranka, & Sanders-Bush, 1981; Conn & Sanders-Bush, 1986; Quick & Azmitia, 1983).

Another method of studying 5-HT in the brain has been by examining a hormone response (prolactin) to a challenge with a 5-HT probe, e.g. with fenfluramine hydrochloride. Fenfluramine increases 5-HT system activity indirectly leading to the release of prolactin. Patients with various disorders such as borderline personality disorder, a history of suicide attempts, or episodic alcohol abuse exhibit reduced prolactin responses to this challenge compared with normal controls (Coccaro et al., 1989; Siever et al., 1987). Recently a similar association between reduced cortisol responses to d-fenfluramine and the motor aggression factor on the BDHI has been found in healthy males (Cleare & Bond, 1997). Another study measured the prolactin response to a challenge with a post-synaptic 5-HT agonist, m-chlorophenylpiperazine (m-CPP) in men with antisocial personality disorder with substance abuse compared with healthy controls (Moss, Yao, & Panzak, 1990). They found that assaultive aggression, resentment, and irritability were associated with a diminished prolactin response to m-CPP. This work therefore confirms the correlation between reduced indices of 5-HT function and irritable, impulsive aggression.

The serotonin system is also affected by drugs leading to disinhibition, impulsivity, and aggression. Alcohol and benzodiazepines may produce behavioural dyscontrol in normal subjects. Although both these substances have effects on a range of neurotransmitter systems, a change in serotonin function could contribute to their disinhibitory effects. Moreover, a relationship between impulsive violent behaviour, low serotonin turnover, and type II alcoholism (i.e. male-linked alcoholism, inherited from fathers by sons, cf. Cloninger, Bohman, & Sigvardsson, 1981) has been found (Linnoila & Virkkunen, 1992; Roy, Virkkunen, & Linnoila, 1987).

In summary, there is animal evidence that many neurotransmitter systems may be involved in aggressive behaviour. In humans the current evidence supports a strong link between affective aggression and lowered levels of central serotonin, although other neuro-transmitter systems are likely to be involved. Recent evidence suggests an associated increase in noradrenergic activity. In addition, studies have shown that these biological correlates of aggressive behaviour are under partial genetic control. Thus, heredity accounts for a significant proportion of the variation in biogenic amines in rhesus monkeys (Clarke et al., 1995). There were significant differences between sire-family groups for CSF levels of noradrenaline, the serotonin metabolite, 5-HIAA, and the dopamine metabolites, HVA and DOPAC. Indirect measures have been used to confirm these results in humans. Reduced prolactin responses to fenfluramine challenge have been found in the relatives of patients with personality disorder and a history of impulsive aggression (Coccaro, Silverman, Klar, Horvath, & Siever, 1994).

HORMONES

The consistency of sex differences in aggressive behaviour across species has led to the study of hormonal influences. The relationship between aggressive and criminal behaviour in men and the sex hormone testosterone has been explored. This hormone appears to be related to some indicators of aggression, but not others. In one study, testosterone levels in prison inmates covaried closely with the violence of the crime for which the inmate had been sentenced, but was not correlated with rated violence of the individuals (Dabbs, Frady, Carr, & Besch, 1987). Testosterone level may be related primarily to a disposition to aggress, and other stimuli must be present before the disposition is manifested in aggressive behaviour. Although testosterone level in boys has been shown to correlate positively to measures of both physical and verbal aggression (Olweus, Mattson, Schalling, & Low, 1980, 1988), the correlation was higher when provocation or threat were examined. Also, a positive correlation was found between testosterone level and lack of tolerance for frustration. At present there is no compelling evidence that testosterone is a direct cause of aggression, but it should be considered as part of a biosocial model (Mazur, 1995).

In women the relation between sex hormones and aggression is unclear. Increased irritability and hostility leading to aggression prior to menstruation have been reported in some studies. Dalton (1977) found a tendency for aggressive behaviour among women inmates during menstruation. In these cases, aggressiveness would be related to a drop in progesterone level during menstruation, along with a rise in the ratio between oestrogen and progesterone. Moreover, administration of progesterone decreased the likelihood of aggressive behaviours during menstruation by alleviating the feelings of irritability and hostility (Dalton, 1977). On the other hand, this associated effect was not confirmed in several other studies, and Bancroft and Backstrom (1985) argue against a direct cause–effect relationship between pre-menstrual mood change and levels of progesterone. Recently, modulation of both the serotonergic and dopamine systems has been reported (Wieck, 1996).

Summing up the evidence, the biological make-up of both humans and animals undoubtedly plays a crucial role as a background condition in the appearance of aggressive behaviours. The data reviewed here suggest that these body chemicals are not in themselves causes of aggression. Aggressive reactions are most likely to result from interactions between external stimuli and personal sensitivities.

DRUGS USED IN THE MANAGEMENT OF AGGRESSION

The laboratory work reviewed earlier is complemented by the empirical assessment of various drugs with a wide range of actions that have been used to treat aggressive behaviour.

Antipsychotics

The antipsychotics are the most used group of compounds, and the treatment of choice for controlling aggression in schizophrenia (Yudofsky, Silver, & Schneider, 1987). Many compounds have been used and their efficacy in controlling rather than treating aggressive behaviour was established in many early studies in the 1960s and 1970s (Itil & Wadud, 1975). A review some years ago suggested that chlorpromazine and trifluopromazine were the most effective of the phenothiazines (Levanthal & Brodie, 1981). Of the other groups, haloperidol is often used unless a depot formulation is required, when flupenthixol decanoate has been shown to be effective. Newer compounds have also been tried with some degree of success (Tuason, 1986). The rationale behind use of these drugs to control aggression is often pragmatic, weighing risks against side-effects, rather than comparing efficacy. It seems that thioridazine, chlorpromazine, and haloperidol are all commonly used in the USA and the UK (Wressell, Tyrer, & Berney, 1990; Yudofsky, Silver, & Hales, 1990) but it is difficult to establish differences between compounds as they have rarely been compared in controlled trials with properly matched samples. Antipsychotics are also used to control acute episodes of disturbed behaviour whatever the pathology. This is termed Rapid Tranquillisation and is primarily a sedative effect (Pilowsky, Ring, Shine, & Lader, 1992).

Although most studies have focused on the use of antipsychotics to control aggressive behaviour in schizophrenia, their efficacy has also been shown in other disorders. It is interesting that antipsychotics including thiothixene and haloperidol have proved helpful in treating impulsiveness and aggressive outbursts in both borderline and impulsive and antisocial personality disorder in low doses, where no obvious tranquillisation is present (Goldberg et al., 1986; Soloff et al., 1986, 1989, 1993; Tyrer & Seivewright, 1988). This group of drugs is also widely used in patients with learning disabilities, and apart from early studies, two more recent studies have shown improvements. One (Gualtieri & Schroeder, 1989) used low-dose (2–8mg) fluphenazine and found a decrease in both self-injury and aggression. The other found pipothiazine palmitate (a depot phenothiazine) to reduce aggression (Lynch, Eliatamby, & Anderson, 1985). Some antipsychotics have also been evaluated in patients with organic brain disease but the improvement in symptoms such as hostility and uncooperativeness is usually only modest (Coccaro et al., 1990). Antipsychotics must be used cautiously in epilepsy or related conditions as these drugs lower the seizure threshold.

Benzodiazepines

Benzodiazepines have been much used in the past in the control of aggressive behaviour, with many studies demonstrating their efficacy (Bond & Lader, 1979). The use of benzodiazepines has also been advocated in the control of acute behavioural disturbance (Mendoza, Djenderedjian, Adams, & Ananth, 1987). This has met with some well-founded criticism (Graham, 1988) but benzodiazepines are often used in conjunction with antipsychotics in rapid tranquillisation (Pilowsky et al., 1992; Salzman, 1988). The anti-aggressive efficacy of benzodiazepines apart from sedation has never been established and recently evidence has been accruing of their pro-aggressive properties. Reports of rage reactions stem from early marketing days, but it was always considered to be a paradoxical response and associated with high doses in predisposed individuals. However, it has been suggested that it may be much more common than hitherto realised and may represent an under-reported general rise in irritability sometimes leading to uncontrolled aggressive outbursts (DiMascio, Shader, & Harmatz, 1969). One review (Dietch & Jennings, 1988) estimated that less than 1% of patients treated with benzodiazepines experienced aggressive dyscontrol.

Animal studies have shown both anti- and pro-aggressive actions for benzodiazepines. These drugs may merely strengthen the current or prevailing behavioural tendency (Dantzer, 1977), but this does not explain why people supposedly behave out of character and may do the same when rechallenged despite the apparent prevailing mood at the time (Regestein & Reich, 1985). Mos and Olivier (1987) conclude from a review of the pro-aggressive effects of benzodiazepines, mainly in animals, that benzodiazepines enhance aggression when basal levels are low to moderate. This may be true of studies in anxious or neurotic patients and in laboratory models used in normal subjects (Gardos, Di Mascio, Salzman, & Shader, 1968; Salzman et al., 1974; Wilkinson, 1985), but does not apply when they are used to treat aggressive behaviour *per se*. Two or three reports have detailed the incidence of hostility following a newer high-potency benzodiazepine, alprazolam, in different patient groups. In one study, 8 out of 80 patients treated with this benzodiazepine displayed extreme anger or hostile behaviour (Rosenbaum, Woods, Groves, & Klerman, 1984). The initial hostility occurred within the first week in all patients and after a single dose in two. Discontinuing the drug led to a resolution of symptoms within a few hours. Three patients were rechallenged and two of the three became hostile. The authors conclude that alprazolam-induced hostility is an early and idiosyncratic effect and may be more likely in patients with well-suppressed chronic anger and resentment.

It should be noted here that triazolam, a high-potency benzodiazepine hypnotic, was withdrawn from the UK market because of problems with adverse reactions including disinhibition and aggression (*Drug and Therapeutics Bulletin*, 1991). Considering this evidence, it would seem advisable to avoid benzodiazepines in the treatment of aggression, but this may be premature as there appear to be differences among compounds: Thus, oxazepam has not been shown to increase aggressive behaviour in normal subjects (Gardos et al., 1968) and has been recommended as a specific anti-hostility tranquilliser (Salzman, Kochansky, Shader, Harmatz, & Ogletree, 1975).

Lithium
In psychiatric patients, most evidence for the efficacy of lithium in the control of aggressive behaviour comes from case studies and uncontrolled reports. A consistent improvement over previous treatments, e.g. the use of phenothiazines or benzodiazepines for years, clearly reveals the failure of other drugs (Shader, Jackson, & Dodes, 1974). There is convincing evidence for the efficacy of lithium in both explosive and aggressive personality disorder and in violent prisoners with mixed diagnoses. A series of studies in the USA showed a reduction in violent incidents and serious assaults without a dulling of affect (Sheard, 1971, 1975; Sheard, Marini, Bridges, & Wagner, 1976). Despite this seemingly favourable evidence, lithium does not appear to have been studied much in patients with antisocial or borderline personality disorder. This could be because of potential side-effects, but it has been suggested that when administered every second day, lithium maintains efficacy with much reduced side-effects (Mellerup & Plenge, 1990). There is also evidence from retrospective studies that lithium may be useful in patients with learning disabilities. The use of lithium in patients with temporal lobe epilepsy or inter-ictal aggressive behaviour is controversial as one study has shown a deterioration in these patients (Jus, Villeneuve, & Gautier, 1973).

Beta-adrenergic antagonists
Numerous case reports and open studies have established the efficacy of high dose beta-adrenergic antagonists in controlling aggression in patients in whom other medication (antipsychotics, benzodiazepines, antidepressants, anticonvulsants) has failed (Elliott, 1977; Greendyke, Schuster, & Wooton, 1984; Yudofsky, Williams, & Gorman, 1981). This effect has been supported in a few double-blind trials (Greendyke & Kanter, 1986; Greendyke, Kanter, Schuster, Verstreate, & Wooton, 1986) and is particularly true for patients with organic brain disease or injury. It has been speculated that the beta blockers may have a bimodal action,

first in the periphery and second in the CNS, and this is supported by work showing nadolol, a peripherally acting beta blocker, to be as effective as propranolol when added to mesoridazine (Polakoff, Sorgi, & Ratey, 1986). A recent review of studies using beta blockers in people with learning disabilities cautioned that the impressive response rate was based solely on case reports and open clinical trials (Ruedrich, Grush, & Wilson, 1990).

In schizophrenia, beta blockers have been added to maintenance antipsychotic treatment and where this has been done systematically, there has been some evidence of improvement (Sorgi, Ratey, & Polakoff, 1986). Although a more recent study with adjunctive nadolol (80–120mg/day) showed only a trend towards decreased aggression (Alpert et al., 1990), the authors rightly point out that any consistent trend when a drug is added double-blind to a behavioural programme is important in a severely disturbed group of patients. However, beta blockers can elevate the bodily concentrations of some antipsychotics by competing for liver enzymes, and so caution with this combination is advocated (Hanssen et al., 1980; Silver, Yudofsky, Kogan, & Katz, 1986). There is some preliminary work to show that propranolol can be useful in intermittent explosive disorder (426mg/day), although patients preferred carbamazepine and tolerated it better (Mattes, Rosenberg, & Maya, 1984).

Anticonvulsants
Electrical disturbances in the brain have been implicated as a cause of episodic human violent behaviour but anticonvulsants, e.g. phenytoin, have had mixed results in the control of such aggressive behaviour over and above the control of epilepsy. Some open trials have been favourable but controlled trials have not always replicated these results, leading to the view that most anticonvulsants are poorly effective in controlling aggressive behaviour in adults (Eichelman, 1987) or children (Conners, Kramer, Rothschild, Schwartz, & Stone, 1971). However, carbamazepine, which has a mood-stabilising effect in addition to its anticonvulsant action, has shown efficacy in managing aggressive behaviour in various patient groups (Cowdry & Gardner, 1988; Mattes, 1990). Carbamazepine has also been added to antipsychotic treatment in schizophrenics. In a double-blind 15-week crossover study of carbamazepine (200mg three times a day) and placebo, all 11 patients showed some improvement and 5 were markedly clinically better (Neppe, 1983). Another retrospective study showed a reduction in recorded aggressive episodes after carbamazepine treatment (Luchins, 1984), and there are many other open and single-case studies confirming improvement in symptoms such as aggression and hostility. There is no

evidence, however, that carbamazepine is effective in schizophrenics not exhibiting symptoms of dyscontrol. In fact, it may produce deterioration because of a lowering of plasma levels of antipsychotics (Kidron, Averbuch, Klein, & Belmaker, 1985). It has therefore been suggested that the rationale for adjunctive carbamazepine treatment in nonresponsive psychosis should be the presence of target symptomatology such as hostility or affective lability (Neppe, 1988, 1990).

Stimulants and antidepressants

Methylphenidate, dextroamphetamine, and pemoline have all shown some efficacy in the treatment of attention-deficit disorder in children and adolescents (Miczek, 1987) and there is some evidence that this effect is also shown in adults who exhibit persistent symptoms of minimal brain dysfunction (Wender, Reimherr, & Wood, 1981; Wender, Reimherr, Wood, & Ward, 1985). Hyperactivity and poor concentration usually improve with age, but where aggressive behaviour is part of the syndrome, it may worsen. Stimulants have limited therapeutic indications as abuse of stimulants and high-dose intoxication can lead to extreme aggression (Ellinwood, 1971), although this is often secondary to a psychotic paranoid state. Although tricyclic antidepressants generally are not effective in the control of aggression, there is some limited evidence, from open trials, of the efficacy of monoamine oxidase inhibitors in attention-deficit disorder and borderline personality disorder, and as newer selective and reversible inhibitors such as moclobemide are developed, they deserve evaluation in this context.

Effects of serotonergic compounds

Tryptophan, the precursor of serotonin, has some beneficial effects when added to maintenance antipsychotic treatment in schizophrenics who have been convicted of violent crime or exhibited episodes of threatening aggression (Morand, Young, & Ervin, 1983). In another study, it showed an indirect effect by decreasing the need for p.r.n. injectable medication in aggressive psychiatric inpatients (Volavka et al., 1990). Both lithium and carbamazepine enhance 5-HT activity. Propranolol has both $5-HT_1$ and $5-HT_2$ antagonist properties, and although the efficacy of the antipsychotics is generally attributed to their anti-dopaminergic and sedative effects, most also block $5HT_2$ receptors (Glennon, 1990). Indeed, both clozapine and risperidone are very active in this respect.

Serotonin agonists

The prototype, buspirone, has been marketed for the treatment of anxiety in the post-benzodiazepine era, but there is evidence that the later compounds, gepirone, ipsapirone, and flesinoxan, are more specific in their action on serotonin without the additional dopaminergic effects of buspirone. These drugs have also been shown to have some antidepressant effect and may in fact have mood-stabilising qualities in neurotic disorders. Animal work has pointed to the importance of the 5-HT_{1A} and 5-HT_{1B} receptor subtypes in the modulation of aggressive behaviour, and a class of drugs that act specifically on the 5-HT_1 receptor (Sijbesma, Schipper, & De Kloet, 1990), aptly named the Serenics—Eltoprazine and Fluprazine—have been developed for their putative anti-aggressive effects (Rasmussen, Olivier, Raghoebar, & Mos, 1990). These are the first drugs to be specifically developed to treat aggressive behaviour but have not fulfilled their early promise. The 5-HT_{1B} receptor has not been identified in the human brain (Hoyer, Pazos, Probst, & Palacios, 1986) and other animal work has suggested that two serotonin classes of receptor may be differentially involved in the modulation of aggression: stimulation of an inhibitory 5-HT_1 receptor and blockade of the 5-HT_2 receptor (Lindgren & Kantak, 1987). As there is interaction between these two receptors, antagonism of 5-HT_2 may enhance the function of 5-HT_1 (Montgomery & Fineberg, 1989), still implying a major role for the 5-HT_1 receptor in aggression.

The only one of these specific compounds yet to be tested formally in aggression is buspirone. There was a suggestion of a reduction in irritability from the original anxiety studies (Glitz & Pohl, 1991) and a series of case reports on people with developmental disabilities has shown a decrease in aggression and self-injury (Ratey, Sovner, Mikkelsen, & Chmielinski, 1989). This has been confirmed in one double-blind study of aggression and anxiety in six patients with mild to moderate learning disabilities who showed decreased aggressive and self-injurious behaviour after buspirone (up to 45mg) (Ratey, Sovner, Parks, & Rogentine, 1991). Other case studies have shown buspirone to decrease aggressive, hostile, and threatening behaviour in patients with varying diagnoses (Balon, 1990; Colenda, 1988; Levine, 1988; Tiller, 1988).

Serotonin re-uptake inhibitors

The serotonin re-uptake inhibitors, which increase central serotonin indirectly (by blocking re-uptake and altering the availability of 5-HT to one or other receptor) have been marketed as antidepressants, but have also had success in treating obsessive-compulsive disorder, which may itself be linked to impaired impulse control. It has been suggested that they work by inducing a state of indifference to intrusive thoughts (Healy, 1990) and so it is also possible that they will increase the perceived threshold to potential sources of provocation and therefore reduce the likelihood of an impulsive aggressive response. Taken together with the work associating lowered CNS levels of serotonin and impulsive aggression, serotonergic compounds may be exerting a normalising effect on a pre-existing deficiency. Although it has been suggested that the serotonin re-uptake inhibitors are effective on symptoms of impulsivity and irritability associated with panic and anxiety, and evidence is emerging that they decrease the incidence of anger attacks in depressed patients (Rosenbaum et al., 1993), systematic studies of their use to treat aggressive behaviour are only now being conducted. There is some preliminary evidence that citalopram may reduce the frequency of aggressive incidents in chronically violent schizophrenic in-patients (Vartiainen et al., 1995) and that fluoxetine may reduce impulsive aggressive behaviour in patients with borderline personality disorder (Cornelius et al., 1991; Markovitz et al., 1991; Norden, 1989) but more well constructed, double-blind trials are necessary.

SUMMARY

The brain mechanisms currently implicated in aggressive behaviour are the amygdala, the hypothalamus, and the temporal lobe. Most of this work is based on invasive techniques, which intervene in normal CNS functioning, and the growth in noninvasive techniques such as brain imaging is likely to improve our knowledge in this field. Many neurotransmitter systems are involved in aggressive behaviour but work in humans implies a strong link between affective or hostile aggression and lowered central serotonin. An association has also been found with enhanced noradrenergic activity and between testosterone and a lack of tolerance for frustration. Although the biological make-up of humans is important in this context, aggressive behaviour is likely to result from interactions between these and other factors, e.g. external and interpersonal stimuli. Many drugs are used clinically in the management of aggression and these are outlined. Different drugs have proved helpful in different types of aggression. There is some evidence that serotonergic compounds may reduce impulsive, irritable aggression but it is suggested that more well-controlled, double-blind trials are needed to evaluate their efficacy.

CHAPTER THREE

Methods: General approaches and experimental techniques

In this chapter we first set out general methods of measuring aggression and then the experimental approach that we adopted, namely a provocation technique with psychophysiological monitoring. In the second part, we detail the specific experimental measures that we used in the four studies comprising Chapters 4 to 7.

Psychology has been defined as a science in which the main aim is "understanding and explaining the lawfulness of individual functioning in real life" (cf. Magnusson, 1988). There is little dispute that the environment influences the likelihood of certain behaviour in specific situations and that genetic endowments set limits on these potential behaviours. Furthermore, it is widely accepted that additional factors like cognitions, mood states, conflict, and other processes influence the probability of the occurrence of specific behaviours (cf. Kimble, 1989; Magnusson, 1988). There are three main ways of studying any behaviour: to observe it, to ask about it and to manipulate it (see Table 3.1). Research into aggression is particularly problematic because it would be unethical to encourage people to do real harm to one another. Therefore much research concentrates on observing or asking people about their behaviour, although experimental laboratory techniques have also been developed.

TABLE 3.1
Techniques of measuring aggression

Observation	Naturalistic
	Experimental intervention
	Observer scales
Reports	Archival
	Clinical scales
	Trait questionnaires
	Situation-reaction questionnaires
	Projective techniques
Experimental laboratory techniques	Aggression machine
	Dyadic interaction
	Competitive reaction time
	Point subtraction paradigm
	Stooge intervention

OBSERVATION

It is difficult to observe and record aggressive behaviour because of its relative infrequency. This means the observer might have to spend a large amount of time watching alternative behaviours. We also know that a third party (the observer) can influence aggression, the very behaviour that is being observed, merely by being present (see p.9). Because the situation is uncontrolled, it is difficult to determine the specific factors that led to the aggression. Nevertheless, observation can be a valuable approach, particularly in some nonverbal or less verbal groups, e.g. children or those with learning disabilities. The researcher must use rigorous methods to record behaviour, e.g. behaviour is coded into numerous different categories and the occurrence is checked off in short time periods. Much of this research has not, however, been entirely naturalistic. Often experimental approaches are combined with observation. Thus, the researcher may intervene to enhance the probability of aggressive behaviour occurring. This is usually done by using accomplices or stooges. For example, in Bandura's early work on social learning (Bandura, Ross, & Ross, 1963), young children were shown an adult accomplice assaulting a large inflatable doll, then placed in a room with toys that included a similar doll, and the children's behaviour was observed and recorded. In work with adults, an accomplice deliberately pushed into a queue that had already formed (Harris, 1973). Pushing into a long queue near the front usually resulted in some form of aggressive behaviour, e.g. threatening or abusive comments, gestures, or pushes, from the other queuers.

These kinds of procedure have provided us with some useful information about aggressive behaviour. However, there are some inherent problems. Observation may be influenced by bias or expectation. Independent observers may disagree on the classification of a particular behaviour. Subjects do not know they are participating in an experiment and so cannot give informed consent. The latter is particularly important with intervention studies. Moreover, the procedures employed may result in real danger to either the accomplice or other participants. These factors must be carefully considered by the experimenter.

Observer scales

In an attempt to standardise the techniques of observation, various clinical scales have been constructed. Two of the most commonly used are the Overt Aggression Scale (Yudofsky, Silver, Jackson, Endicott, & Williams, 1986), which scores both verbal and physical aggression as well as the need for staff intervention, and the Nurses' Observation Scale for Inpatient Evaluation (Honigfeld, Gillies, & Klett, 1976), which was developed specifically for nurses to score aggressive behaviour on the ward. Recently a group of European clinicians held a meeting to construct another specific aggression scale (European Rating Aggression Group, 1992). The Social Dysfunction and Aggression Scale measures two independent dimensions: inward and outward aggression. This scale does not only record obvious violence and assaults but also includes a range of aggressiveness from irritability and dysphoria to more directed verbal and physical aggression (Wistedt et al., 1990).

REPORTS

Perhaps the easiest and therefore most widely used method of gathering information about aggressive behaviour is some form of report. In some cases, archival data is used to try and link external variables with behaviour, e.g. a rise in temperature with rioting in the streets. In other cases rating scales may be used. Many clinical scales have items to measure hostility and aggression (e.g. Brief Psychiatric Rating Scale, Overall & Gorham, 1962). These scales mainly record behaviour over a certain period of time, so the respondent is asked about the last month, for example, although the behaviour may be habitual. Data on the usual form of responding may also be obtained verbally by interview or from someone acquainted with the subject who may be asked to rate the usual behaviour pattern or personality characteristics of the subject. Usually, however, self-reports are used. These can be personality inventories, mood ratings, or attitude questionnaires. Various measures have been developed to investigate aspects of hostility, anger, and aggression.

Trait and state questionnaires

Measures of hostility

Trait questionnaires aim to measure how a subject usually feels or behaves. Many of these have been derived from wider personality inventories. For example, numerous hostility scales were developed from the Minnesota Multiphasic Personality Inventory (MMPI) in the 1950s and 1960s, e.g. the Cook and Medley Hostility Scale, the Iowa Hostility Scale, the Manifest Hostility Scale. These scales are termed "intuitive" by Edmunds and Kendrick (1980), where a comprehensive discussion can be found, because items were selected according to face or content validity. Most of them have now fallen into disuse because they did not discriminate between groups theoretically expected to differ on aggression, and showed only limited construct validity. The Manifest Hostility Scale (Siegal, 1956; Siegal, Spilka, & Miller, 1957) has been used in various experimental studies. High scorers have been found to be more aggressive under conditions of provocation (Edmunds & Kendrick, 1980) but the scale was shown to be confounded by social desirability. Other studies have not found the scale to discriminate between hostile and nonhostile groups in clinical settings.

Some scales with items chosen from the MMPI have derived them on an empirical basis. Thus, Schultz (1954) administered the MMPI to patients who had been rated by psychotherapists on 5 dimensions of aggression. From this data, he produced a 55-item scale with 3 subscales: overt aggression, covert aggression, and control of hostility. However, in further studies, this scale has also failed to discriminate between assaultive and nonassaultive groups.

Megargee et al. (1967) also derived items from the MMPI for their Overcontrolled Hostility Scale (O-HS). They used a series of item analyses of the MMPI protocols of assaultive and nonassaultive subjects to construct the scale based on their theory of overcontrolled versus undercontrolled aggression (see p.19). They conducted many studies to test the scale's validity and found that extremely assaultive criminals did have higher scores on the O-HS as they predicted. This scale would seem to have rather limited applications and Megargee (1969) recommends that it be used with other social, clinical, and personality information as a strong inhibition of aggression does not necessarily indicate the risk of extreme violence in a normal population.

Measures of hostility and aggression

Some other scales have been derived according to a particular psychological theory of aggression. The Hostility and Direction of Hostility Questionnaire (HDHQ) (Caine, Foulds, & Hope, 1967) is based on Foulds' (1965) theory that aggression is a drive with two main forms of expression: extrapunitiveness and intropunitiveness. A principal components analysis revealed a general hostility dimension and a direction of hostility dimension. Some work in clinical samples has shown paranoid patients to be more extrapunitive than neurotic patients, and those with severe personality disorders to obtain similar scores to those of psychotic patients on the general hostility dimension. In general, scores are higher in patients with more severe psychiatric disorder. The HDHQ has also been shown to have some predictive validity for post-natal depression when administered during the first trimester of pregnancy and has been shown to be sensitive to change after drug treatment of various disorders (Priest, Tanner, Gandhi, & Bhandari, 1995).

The Buss–Durkee Hostility Inventory (BDHI) is based on psychological theory of different types of aggression (Buss & Durkee, 1957). The authors first distinguished between aggression as a behaviour and hostility as an enduring attitude and subdivided them. They subdivided aggression and hostility according to 8 subtypes (see Table 3.2) and constructed a pool of 105 items, each of which was thought to refer to only one subclass, was specific, and which minimised defensiveness and therefore social desirability. They attempted to construct an equal number of items to be scored true or false but found that it was only plausible to have a 3:1 ratio. After administering the inventory to a sample of college students, the number of items was reduced to 75. All 8 subscales were kept and a factor analysis revealed two factors with 4 scales on one and 2 on the other (see Table 3.2). However, the factor loadings were not high, indicating unique variance

TABLE 3.2
Factor structure of Buss–Durkee Hostility Inventory

Motor aggression	*Attitudinal hostility*
Assault	Resentment
Verbal hostility	Suspicion
Irritability	
Indirect hostility	
(Negativism)	(Guilt)

for several scales. The test-retest reliability was found to be 0.82 for the total scale but negativism had weak stability (0.46). Several researchers have found that the BDHI correlates with other measures of hostility (Baron & Richardson, 1994). Component analyses conducted on the inventory have largely supported the original scoring (Edmunds & Kendrick, 1980; Velicer, Govia, Cherico, & Corriveau, 1985). Other modifications, e.g. a seven-choice response format, have resulted in changes in the structure (Buss & Perry, 1992; Velicer et al., 1985) but have been little used to date. Edmunds and Kendrick (1980) found stable factors similar to the original for male subjects. They found the aggression factor to discriminate between people otherwise rated high and low in aggressiveness but not to their willingness to direct electric shocks to another subject, i.e. their performance on the Buss Aggression Machine (see p.53). However, other studies have shown extreme scorers on the BDHI to differ on the number and intensity of shocks given in retaliation for shocks received (Knott, 1970), i.e. under conditions of provocation. The BDHI has also been shown to discriminate between violent and nonviolent alcohol abusers (Renson, Adams, & Tinklenberg, 1978) and prisoners (Lothstein & Jones, 1978).

Measures of anger

Other investigators have focused on measures of anger. These scales are too numerous to detail here so only a few will be mentioned. Spielberger and colleagues have developed two scales. The State-Trait Anger Scale (Spielberger, Jacobs, Russell, & Crane, 1983) measures both a temporary emotion and a more stable personality trait. The Anger Expression Scale (Spielberger et al., 1985) measures both the total extent of anger and whether it is expressed (out) or suppressed (in). The Multidimensional Anger Inventory (Siegel, 1986) was developed to study the role of anger in cardiovascular disease. The scale measures different dimensions of anger, such as arousal, hostile outlook, anger-in, anger-out, as well as a range of situations that may provoke anger. Novaco in his Anger Inventory also examines how angry people become (Novaco, 1975). Subjects are presented with 90 situations and have to rate anger for each on a five-point scale. High scores indicate anger proneness.

Concurrent validity has been demonstrated for these scales, i.e. they correlate with other measures of anger or hostility. One problem is that the way many of the scales have been developed results in an overlap of items from one scale to another. It seems likely that trait anger is similar to attitudinal hostility, although the Trait Anger Scale (Spielberger et al., 1983) includes items relating to physical and verbal aggression, e.g. when I get frustrated, I feel like hitting someone; when I get annoyed,

I say nasty things. The measurement of anger may then be confounded by different types of aggressive feelings and behaviour.

A simpler way in which to measure state feelings of anger or hostility might be to use visual analogue scales (VAS). VAS have been shown to be a reliable and valid way of measuring current feelings or emotions, e.g. depression and anxiety (Bond, Shine, & Bruce 1995; McCormack, Horne, & Sheather, 1988). They are simple, easy and quick to construct, administer and score and particularly useful when repeated measures are required at short time intervals. We have constructed a 13-item scale (see Fig. 3.1) to measure feelings of anger and have previously found this scale to be sensitive to task-induced changes (Bond & Lader, 1986).

Situation reaction questionnaires

Another method that has been used to measure the reporting of aggressive behaviour is to give subjects a number of scenarios and ask them to report how they would feel and what they would do. This sort of technique has shown that "psychopaths" are more likely to perceive any threatening (anxiety or anger) scenario as more anger-provoking (Blackburn & Lee-Evans, 1985; Sterling & Edelmann, 1988). The Anger Situation Questionnaire (van Goozen, Frijda, Kindt, & van de Poll, 1994) has been developed specifically to measure anger proneness in women. This disposition is measured in terms of rated emotion, intensity of the emotion felt, and action readiness. The Conflict Tactics Scale (Steinmetz, 1977) was specifically designed to examine violence in the family. In it, respondents are asked to indicate the type of behaviour in which members of their family have engaged in order to solve a problem. A list of increasingly violent behaviour is given and these are rated on a five-point scale. These questionnaires can be useful in eliciting common methods of responding to frustration or provocation and may isolate problem areas.

Projective techniques

In contrast to asking subjects directly about their feelings and actions, a totally different approach has been to use projective techniques to measure them indirectly. The subject is presented with ambiguous stimuli such as ink-blots (Rorschach Inkblot Test) or indistinct pictures (Thematic Apperception Test) and asked to describe them or write about them in some way. It is assumed that subjects will "project" their motives, needs, or conflicts through their responses and these can be interpreted or scored by the experimenter. In fact, the scoring is the most difficult task to accomplish and this makes the reliability of such techniques questionable. Nevertheless, there is evidence that people with a history of aggressive behaviour produce responses with more

Name: .... Age: .... Date: .... Sex: ....

1. Please rate the way you feel in terms of the dimensions given below
2. Regard the line as representing the full range of each dimension
3. Rate your feelings as they are AT THE MOMENT
4. Mark clearly and perpendicularly across each line

ANGRY	_____	PEACEFUL
AFFABLE	_____	QUARRELSOME
FURIOUS	_____	CALM
SOCIABLE	_____	UNSOCIABLE
AGGRESSIVE	_____	COOL-HEADED
BELLIGERENT	_____	RESTRAINED
RESENTFUL	_____	TOLERANT
PATIENT	_____	IMPATIENT
FRIENDLY	_____	HOSTILE
SPITEFUL	_____	BENEVOLENT
ANNOYED	_____	COMPOSED
PLEASED	_____	DISGUSTED
REBELLIOUS	_____	COMPLIANT

FIG. 3.1. Anger rating scale (not to scale).

hostile content on the Rorschach Inkblot Test (Buss, 1961). Much of this work was done before 1970 and in a review at that time Megargee (1970) concluded that if such techniques were to be helpful in discriminating between people, they had to be used in a uniform and consistent way to make any results replicable. The Rosenweig Picture-Frustration Test was developed as a semiprojective technique with scoring categories (Rosenweig, 1981) but it has not proved to be any more reliable than the other techniques.

EXPERIMENTAL LABORATORY TECHNIQUES

Investigation of human aggression in a systematic experimental fashion began with the publication of the monograph *Frustration and Aggression* (Dollard et al., 1939). This stimulated a lot of research on the effects of frustration on aggressive behaviour. The next major influence was the introduction of laboratory experiments in the early 1960s with Arnold Buss' (1961) technique for measuring aggression. This is presented as a teaching situation. The subjects are told that they are participating with another subject (an accomplice of the experimenter) in a study on the effects of punishment on learning. They, as teacher, will notify the other subject of correct or incorrect responses on a task by administering a shock. This is done via an apparatus that has come to be known as the "aggression machine". The level of shock that can be administered varies from very mild (button 1) to an extremely powerful jolt (button 10) and the subject is free to choose the level they think appropriate. In actuality, the accomplice does not receive any shock. The procedure results in three measures of aggression: the shock intensity selected; the average shock duration administered; and a composite measure obtained by multiplying the two. This aggression machine has been employed in numerous studies and there is some evidence that behaviour on the machine indicates the strength of subjects' tendencies to harm others (Baron & Richardson, 1994). Despite these findings, some investigators have presented evidence that subjects may administer shocks to help the accomplice or confederate to learn (Rule & Leger, 1976), and thus the results are very dependent on the instructions given and the beliefs of the subject. Refinements to the original Buss (1961) technique have tried to address these problems (Gustafson, 1992) and have concluded that valid data can be obtained if careful manipulation checks are included.

A slightly different technique, but also using shock and the dyadic situation of subject–confederate, is that devised by Berkowitz (1962, 1964). The subjects are told that they will participate in an experiment concerned with the effects of stress on problem-solving ability. The subject is required to provide a written solution to a problem (posed by the experimenter), which will be evaluated by the partner (confederate) by the administration of a shock. In this paradigm, the level of shock is predetermined, an intervening variable is interposed, e.g. a violent or nonviolent film, and then the subject and partner change positions. This procedure results in one or two measures of aggression: the number of shocks set by the subject and sometimes the duration, but the intensity is preset. Many variations of this procedure have been used, and in both the Buss and Berkowitz procedures, provoked subjects behave more aggressively.

In a third laboratory technique devised by Taylor (1967) the subject takes part in a competition on a simple reaction time task with a real or putative opponent. The slower reactor on each trial receives an electric shock set by the opponent (intensity 1–10). In fact, the number of trials lost and the intensity of shocks set for the subject are predetermined. The measure of aggression is the intensity of the shocks set by the subject and this can be seen as two measures. The first trial represents unprovoked aggression and the rest of the trials retaliative behaviour. This procedure offers advantages over those of Buss (1961) and Berkowitz (1962). The victim is not helpless but can retaliate, and as the victim is actually a confederate, the victim's behaviour can be systematically varied to investigate the effects. Thus, the effects of numerous different manipulations have been explored on this paradigm, from task variables, i.e. the pattern of shocks given (Bernstein, Richardson, & Hammock, 1987; O'Leary & Dengerink, 1973; Pisano & Taylor, 1971), to external variables, i.e. the effects of third-party instigation to aggress (Gaebelein & Hay, 1975), or the effects of alcohol (Richardson, 1981; Shuntich & Taylor, 1972). There is some evidence of the validity of this procedure. Subjects who rate themselves as undercontrolled respond more aggressively than those who are overcontrolled (Taylor, 1967), and one study comparing the aggression machine and the competitive RT task found performance on the two to correlate, especially under conditions of no or low provocation (Bernstein et al., 1987). Subjects theoretically expected to differ in aggressive potential also show differences on the task-derived measure of aggression (Dengerink, 1971; Genthner & Taylor, 1973).

Several other experimental laboratory techniques have been used in aggression research. Zeichner and Pihl (1979) modified the aggression machine to examine specifically the effects of alcohol. Subjects were subjected to aversive tones, the intensity of which was either correlated or not with the shocks they delivered. A point subtraction aggression paradigm (PSAT) has been developed (Cherek, 1981), again based on a dyadic interaction. On this task subjects are provided with two or three button-pressing response options. Pressing button A a number of times (N = 100) results in the earning of one point, which represents a monetary reward. Pressing button B (N = 10) results in the subtraction of one point from another subject, and button C (N = 10) in a blast of white noise being delivered to the other subject. In later experiments (Kelly & Cherek, 1993), the noise option has been abandoned and in some an "escape" option has been allowed, i.e. protection of points already earned for a short period of time. Subjects are provoked to respond "aggressively" by having points subtracted from them, this action being attributed to the other person. Verbal measures of hostility to stimuli are believed to resemble physical aggressive responses (Berkowitz, 1962; Berkowitz & Geen, 1967). Thus, instead of administering shocks, subjects may be required to give a verbal message to their opponent. However, Baron (1977) suggested a distinction between those investigations in which the subjects' evaluations of another person can potentially inflict harmful consequences on that person (e.g. Berkowitz, Corwin, & Heironimus, 1962) and those in which they can not. The former would be considered as an expression of aggression, whereas the latter would be expression of subjects' current emotional arousal.

Several of these experimental techniques use confederates or accomplices of the experimenter to act as the other competitor or aggressor, but sometimes a stooge is used to behave in a certain way. The subject is set a task to accomplish and the stooge is introduced to provoke the subject by means of interference, delay, or harassment (Erdmann & van Lindern, 1980; Netter, Janke, & Erdman, 1995). This kind of provocation has also been used in groups, i.e. a group rather than an individual is set a task, then told that the result is inadequate and they must start again (Salzman et al., 1974). The consequent interaction is scored by Bales Interaction Process Analysis (Bales, 1950).

An extensive literature has accumulated on bargaining games and some of these studies have been linked conceptually with aggression research (e.g. Pisano & Taylor, 1971; Tedeschi, Gaes, & Rivera, 1977).

Certain components therefore seem to be important in laboratory techniques. Tasks based on an interpersonal competition in which either the subject or the opponent can win or lose elicit more aggression than aggressor/victim-based tasks. Provocation is an important factor and should preferably be incorporated into the task. Aggressive behaviour is dependent on the subject's understanding of and beliefs about the task and so careful manipulation checks should be conducted.

Psychophysiological measures

Arousal is not a unitary concept in either psychophysiology or psychology (cf. Gale & Edwards, 1983). The arousal basis of a theory of social behaviour is demonstrable physiologically only if arousal is specified in biological terms. The usual implicit use of arousal and its referents (tension, stress, dissonance, and so on) serves often as a symbolic rather than psychophysiological construct (Averill, 1974). According to dissonance theory (Festinger, 1957), opposing cognitions generate psychic tension, leading to behavioural or attitudinal changes. However, as discussed in the previous chapters, affective aggression is usually accompanied by distinctive physiological changes (Johansson, 1981). These can be measured by self-report, but a much more direct way is to use psychophysiological monitoring.

Psychophysiological research on arousal has concentrated on autonomic nervous system activity, particularly electrodermal and cardiovascular responses. The electrical activity of the skin is due to eccrine sweat gland activity. The sympathetic nervous system is the common pathway to the eccrine sweat glands from the CNS areas that control arousal as well as motor activity, emotional behaviour, homeostatic function, and attention (Fowles, 1986). The activation of sympathetic nerves releases the neurotransmitter acetylcholine, which stimulates cholinergic receptors on the sweat glands, causing them to secrete sweat into coiled sweat ducts. This sympathetic mediated secretion of sweat is detected at the skin surface as an electrodermal response (Lader & Montagu, 1962), with the response size depending primarily on the degree of the duct-filling. Some sweat is absorbed by the skin, contributing to variations in electrodermal level and response size (Fowles, 1986). Electrodermal activity (EDA) is typically recorded on the surface of the palms and soles where the concentration of eccrine sweat glands is greatest. There the sweat gland activity, whose primary function is to maintain adequate moisture levels in the outer layer of the skin to improve abrasion resistance and enhance tactile sensitivity, is also involved in thermoregulation under some circumstances (Fowles, 1986). Considering that these effects are adaptative in situations requiring fight or flight, an increase in EDA is a prominent feature of the sympathetically mediated defence reaction (fight–flight response). Electrodermal responses are also an integral part of the orienting reaction to novel or significant stimuli (Graham & Clifton, 1966).

Cardiovascular activity, like EDA, is regulated by CNS pathways governing motor activity, emotional reactions, homeostatic function, attention, and arousal. The autonomic nervous system also provides the common pathway from these central systems to the heart and the vasculature (Larsen, Schneiderman, & Pasin, 1986). Neural control occurs by complex nervous system interactions (Obrist, 1981). Parasympathetic effects on the heart are mediated by cholinergic transmission involving acetylcholine released by the vagus nerve, while sympathetic effects are mediated by beta-adrenergic transmission involving noradrenaline released by the cardiac sympathetic nerves. Myocardial beta-adrenergic receptors are also sensitive to circulating adrenaline released by the adrenal medulla on sympathetic activation (Larsen et al., 1986).

For assessment purposes laboratory-based aggression research should use psychophysiological measures as well as questionnaires and self-reports. Physiological changes accompanying anger can be measured even if overt aggressive behaviour does not alter much.

Experimental techniques
A range of psychological and psychophysiological methods was used and they are all described later. However, not every technique was used in all of the studies described in Chapters 4 to 7. The competitive reaction time task and certain subjective rating scales were, however, common to all the studies.

Experimental situation and design
The competitive reaction time task used was a modification of that designed by Taylor (1967). It was not thought ethical to use shocks, especially with patient populations, and so white noise of increasing intensity was substituted. We have found healthy volunteer subjects both to escalate their behavioural aggression in response to provocation during this procedure (Bond & Lader, 1986) and to rate increased anger.

Competitive reaction time task
The subjects were told that they were engaged in a competitive reaction time task with a subject in another room. The subjects were instructed to adjust a switch on the task box at the beginning of each trial so that any of 8 intensities of noise could be delivered (see Fig. 3.2). There were 8 levels at 5db increments with 70db having a score of 1 and 105db a score of 8. These noises, they were informed, would be administered to their opponent at the end of the trial if their reaction time was faster than their opponent's; their opponent had similar privileges. Thus, the subjects realised that they might hear or administer a noise depending on the outcome of the competition and the magnitude of the noise could be varied by both competitors. In fact there was no opponent.

The level of provocation (noise level administered to the subject) was increased through the experiment. After the initial (no provocation) trial, the 24 trials were divided into 4 blocks of 6 trials each. (In some

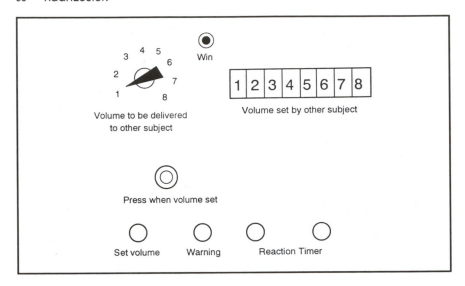

FIG. 3.2. Illustration of front of task box used for the competitive reaction time task.

studies only 18 trials, and therefore 3 blocks, were used.) On the first block, the noise level averaged 1.5. There were three trials at level 1 and three trials at level 2 administered in random order. On the second block the noise level averaged 3.5, and on the third and fourth 5.5 and 7.5, respectively. The subject heard the actual noise on half the occasions within each block, irrespective of RT performance. However, in order to keep the competition realistic, the programme was designed where possible to administer a noise if the subject's RT was 20% or more slower than the subject's running average, and not to administer a noise if the RT was 20% faster than average. The noise was administered through headphones and lasted between 0.5 and 2 seconds according to a predetermined order, so that the average length of noise within each block was the same. When the subject won the trial, a win button was illuminated and the subject had to depress this button for the length of time s/he wanted to administer the noise. There was an upper limit of 5 seconds. (This option was only available in some studies.)

Procedure

All subjects received 25 or 19 trials. Each trial contained the same sequence of events.

1. Green light on—signal for subject to set the level of noise for the opponent.
2. Green button—subject presses when ready to proceed.

3. Light display on—one of a number of lights (1–8) was illuminated to display the level of noise set by the opponent.
4. Amber light on—warning for RT stimulus.
5. Red light on—RT stimulus.
6. Red button—subject presses in response.
7. Noise—administered on half of the trials.

The time interval between events 1 and 2 was totally dependent on the subject. The length of each trial was a minimum of 50sec and averaged 54sec and so the total time for the task was approximately 20min.

The data from the 25 (or 19) trials were summarised by a pre-score (trial 1) and 4 (or 3) subsequent scores, each representing the mean of 6 trials. A laboratory computer controlled the task box and recorded the psychophysiological variables.

Physiological measures

Heart period

The heart period was monitored throughout the experiment. Conventional ECG electrodes were strapped to the lower left forearm and lower left leg after preparing the electrode sites by abrasion and the application of Neptic electrode gel. The ECG was amplified and the inter-beat interval (IBI) recorded. During each trial a set number of IBIs was measured between the significant events (see Table 3.3). The mean of each of these was taken and these figures were averaged for blocks of 6 trials giving a pre-score (trial one) and 4 (or 3) other readings.

TABLE 3.3
Heart period related to the events within trials

Events	Heart period (IBIs)
Pre-trial	Recorded 10
Post-ready button pressed	Recorded 10
Post-volume display on	Recorded 3
Post-amber light	Recorded 3
Post-reaction time	Recorded 3
Post-noise (50%)	Recorded 3
Post-win light (50%)	Recorded 3

Skin conductance level
The palmar skin conductance was recorded throughout the experiment using a constant voltage method (Contact Precision Instruments Skin Conductance Module). Silver/silver chloride electrodes were applied to the distal segments of the first two fingers of the left hand. K.Y. jelly was used as the conductive medium. The output of the module was sampled by the computer and also recorded using a polygraph. Two readings were taken within each trial at the beginning (pre-Green Light) and at the point of greatest change within the trial. The latter was expressed as a difference score from the pre-trial level. The initial reading and the difference score were averaged across the 4 (or 3) blocks of trials. The number of fluctuations greater than a certain criterion (0.04 microsiemens) was counted for 15sec pre-trial, 15sec during the trial and 15sec post-RT.

Subjective ratings

1. Mood Rating Scale (MRS).   The subjects completed a visual analogue mood rating scale of 16 items. For each item the subject had to make a mark along a 100mm line and the score was measured in mm from the scale end to that mark. In addition three factors previously isolated from the scale were analysed (Bond & Lader, 1974). They were alertness, contentment, and calmness.

2. Anger Rating Scale (ARS).   This scale (see Fig. 3.1) consisted of 13 items measuring feelings of anger and hostility and was constructed in a similar way to the MRS (Bond & Lader, 1986).

3. Spielberger State-Trait Anxiety Inventory (STAI).   The STAI-Trait was administered to measure how much anxiety subjects generally felt and the STAI-State required subjects to indicate how they felt "at this moment" (Spielberger, Gorsuch, & Lushene, 1970).

4. Spielberger State-Trait Anger Scale (STAS).   The STAS-Trait was used to measure individual differences in the frequency of experiencing anger and the STAS-State required subjects to indicate how they felt "at this moment" (Spielberger et al., 1983).
    The results for these four scales before the competitive reaction time task and immediately after it are presented.

5. Drinking Questionnaire.   Subjects completed a simple four-question scale on frequency of drinking, amount on each occasion, and the quantity drunk in a usual week and last week.

   6. Conviction Questionnaire.   A five-point questionnaire (Gunn &
Robertson, 1976) was administered to examine convictions related to
violence.

   7. Buss–Durkee Hostility Inventory.   This 75-item inventory (see
Table 3.2) was administered to assess various aspects of aggression and
hostility according to eight subscales: Assault, Indirect hostility,
Irritability, Verbal hostility, Negativism, Resentment, Suspicion, and
Guilt (Buss & Durkee, 1957). The mean of the first four scales
represented the Motor Aggression Factor.

Other physiological measures

Electroencephalogram (EEG)

This was recorded from vertex and left parietal electrodes (C_z and T_3 in
the 10-20 system) using silver/silver chloride electrodes. The amplified
EEG was passed through a 1–30Hz bandpass filter before undergoing a
Fourier transform and power-spectral density analysis. The recording
consisted of 48 epochs of 2sec duration, sampled at 125Hz. Each epoch
was transformed into a power spectrum using a fast Fourier transform
and the average spectrum over 48 epochs computed for the condition
(eyes open). The power spectrum was then condensed into four bands:
2.0–4.0Hz (delta), 4.5–7.5Hz (theta), 8.0–13.0Hz (alpha) and 13.5 Hz to
26.0Hz (beta).

Auditory evoked potential and reaction time

The auditory evoked potentials and auditory reaction time were
measured at the same time. The EEG was recorded between the vertex
and the left ear lobe, using the right ear lobe as the earth reference.
Amplifier half amplitude upper cut-off frequency was set at 100Hz.
Subjects responded to a 70db "click" by pressing a button as quickly as
possible (reaction time). Click stimuli were repeated at random
intervals of between 8 and 12 seconds. The EEG was sampled at 1
millisecond intervals for 350 milliseconds after each click. Thirty-two
epochs of artifact-free EEG were averaged, and four peaks were
identified (P_1, N_1, P_2, and N_2). Their latencies and P_1-N_1, N_1-P_2, and
P_2-N_2 amplitudes were calculated. Similarly, 32 reaction times were
recorded in milliseconds, and the mean reciprocal calculated. For both
auditory evoked potentials and reaction time, the response to the first
click was ignored.

SUMMARY

In this chapter we discussed methods of recording and measuring aggressive behaviour. Fieldwork usually involves observation and can be particularly valuable in nonverbal groups provided that rigorous controls are employed. In some experiments, conditions have been manipulated to enhance the probability of aggression but it is important to consider both the potential danger and the ethical implications of this. Many rating scales have been constructed to measure aggression. Observer scales can be helpful in very disturbed groups but more often self-reports are used. These can be divided into trait questionnaires, which measure stable patterns of aggressive behaviour and hostile feelings, and state scales, which measure current feelings of hostility or anger. Situation reaction questionnaires ask subjects directly how they would behave and feel in a given situation, whereas projective techniques infer hostility from responses to ambiguous stimuli. In order to measure aggression more directly, experimental laboratory techniques have been developed. As aggression occurs within an interpersonal context, techniques have usually modelled a dyadic situation. Much work has centred on the Buss aggression machine, in which the subject is required to administer shocks to another subject (in reality an accomplice of the experimenter) as part of a teaching situation. Careful manipulation checks need to be included because results are very dependent on the instructions given and the beliefs of the subject. Other techniques involve reciprocal aggression. In the competitive reaction time task, the subject takes part in a simple reaction time competition in which either the subject or the opponent may receive or administer a shock depending on the outcome. Although the most common measure of behavioural aggression has been the number or intensity of shocks administered, other tasks have used subtraction of money or verbal messages. In some experiments a stooge has been introduced to provoke the subject by means of delay, interference, or harassment. Emotional arousal often accompanies hostile aggression and so psychophysiological techniques are described. It is difficult to discriminate physiologically between different emotions and therefore these recordings should be used in conjunction with self-reports and behavioural measures. Finally, the experimental techniques employed in this series of studies are described. We modified the competitive reaction time task to use white noise of increasing intensity and monitored cardiac and electrodermal activity during the task. The subjects filled in various trait and state measures of aggression and hostility pre-and post-competing.

CHAPTER FOUR

Behavioural aggression in a clinical group

INTRODUCTION

This study was designed to assess physiological and psychological variables in patients with a history of aggression. Studies of biological correlates of aggression in psychiatric patients have been few, and most concentrate on extremely disturbed patients. In most of these experiments, aggression has been assessed through interviews and questionnaires. The data gathered from such studies are indirect, which hinders making reliable inferences.

One problem in dealing with clinical populations is multiple pathology. Thus, patients with a history of acts of aggression or complaints of hostile feelings tend also to suffer from other abnormal behaviour or affects including anxiety, depression, and obsessive-compulsive behaviour. Some, indeed, display psychotic features. In order to disentangle the aggressive aspects from the others, we used two comparator groups. The first was *healthy normal subjects,* i.e. individuals with neither aggressive nor any other psychiatric problems. The second was a *control group* of patients who had psychiatric abnormalities, mainly clinical anxiety and depression, but had no history of aggressive behaviour. We used the competitive reaction time paradigm as described in the previous chapter. It was hypothesised that the patients with a history of aggression would become more aggressive on provocation than the other two groups.

Methods

Subjects

Forty-eight subjects (42 males, 6 females) participated in the study, comprising three groups of 14 males and 2 females. All groups were matched by sex and age as closely as possible. Patients were also matched by primary diagnosis. One group of patients, the "forensic patients", had a history of physical aggression. Most of these were referred by the Forensic Psychiatry Department of the Maudsley Hospital. The remainder as well as the control patients were recruited through other Maudsley Hospital clinics. Subjects for the normal group were recruited from a local job centre. In the forensic group only one was an in-patient compared with two in the control patient group.

The psychiatric record of each patient was reviewed for diagnosis based on the "International Classification of Diseases, 9th Revision". The psychiatric diagnoses consisted of anxiety disorders (4 forensic, 4 controls), delusional disorders (2 forensics), mood disorders (9 forensic, 12 controls) and personality disorder (1 forensic). However, in reviewing the patients' clinical records, personality disorder was a second-level diagnosis in an additional 11 forensic patients. Two forensic patients had a history of drug abuse, one with marijuana and heroin, and another with marijuana; one had a history of alcohol abuse and three of benzodiazepine dependence. In the control group one patient had a history of benzodiazepine dependence and one had previously abused alcohol. Nine forensic and five control patients had attempted suicide or self-harm—four forensic patients had made suicide attempts more than once. At the time of testing and in the previous two weeks 7 patients in the forensic group were drug-free as compared with 3 in the control group. Six forensic patients were taking one single drug, whereas 3 were taking two drugs simultaneously. In the control group 11 patients were on treatment with one drug and 2 patients were taking two drugs at the same time (see Table 4.1). All normal subjects were drug-free.

Patients with a diagnosis of epilepsy, schizophrenia, or mental handicap were excluded, as well as those with a history of head injury.

Materials and procedures

The procedures were approved by the appropriate Ethical Committee of the Institute of Psychiatry and the Bethlem Royal and Maudsley Hospitals. All subjects were informed about the tests, both physiological and psychological, in a short interview and signed a consent form.

They attended the laboratory on one occasion, always in the afternoons at about 2 pm. Subjects were asked to avoid drinking alcohol

TABLE 4.1
Psychotropic drug frequencies

	Frequency	
	Forensic patients (n = 16)	*Control patients (n = 16)*
Psychotropic drugs		
Anti-anxiety (including sedatives and hypnotics)	6	2
Antidepressants	1	9
Antimanic	1	2
Antipsychotic	2	2
Drugs for movement disorders	1	—
Antihypertensives	1	—

on the night before and the day of testing. They were also asked to consume only a light meal immediately before the testing session. Those patients who were taking medication were requested not to change their treatments in any way.

The experimental session lasted for about 90 minutes and most tests were recorded using a computer. The testing conditions were kept as standard as possible.

The experimenter started each experimental session by interviewing the patient concerning demographic and diagnostic characteristics, followed by a set of questionnaires and subjective rating scales that the patient completed before the recording of the physiological variables was set up. At this stage contact with subjects was friendly but uninformative. Instructions about performing the tests were read in a systematic, controlled way. The sequence of tests is shown in Table 4.2.

Measures

Psychophysiological measures
The psychophysiological variables (EEG, AEP, SC level) were recorded, as described previously, during a simple reaction time task.

Competitive reaction time task
This measure of aggressive behaviour was carried out as described in the previous chapter. The heart period and skin conductance level were monitored during the task.

TABLE 4.2
Test sequence

Time 1:	Consent form
	Conviction questionnaire
	Questionnaire on drinking behaviour
	Mood rating scale
	Anger rating scale
	Spielberger State Anxiety Inventory
	Spielberger Trait Anxiety Inventory
	Spielberger State Anger Scale
	Spielberger Trait Anger Scale
	EEG
	AEP + skin conductance level + reaction time
	CRT—with continuous monitoring of heart rate and skin conductance level
Time 2:	Mood rating scale
	Anger rating scale
	Spielberger State Inventories
	EEG
	AEP + skin conductance level + reaction time
	Buss–Durkee Hostility Inventory

EEG = electroencephalogram; AEP = auditory evoked potential; CRT = competitive reaction time.

Subjective rating scales
The Mood Rating Scale, Anger Rating Scale, and Spielberger State-Trait, Anxiety and Anger Inventories were completed at the beginning and at the end of the recording session. The Conviction Questionnaire, Drinking Questionnaire, and the Buss–Durkee Hostility Inventory were filled in once.

Analysis of data
Parametric statistics were used and included analysis of variance (uni- and multivariate) with repeated measures. Analysis of variance tested for overall differences between the groups and included an analysis to confirm the comparability of the groups. Trend analysis evaluated any task-related effects over time.

Because of the large amount of data, critical differences were used in most instances to indicate the dispersion in the data. Critical difference is the divisor in a between-means t-test and was calculated from the error variance in the overall analysis of variance (least significant difference test). The 0.05 critical difference is plotted on the graphs as a vertical bar, labelled C.D., and any means further apart than this are significantly different at the 0.05 level of probability at least.

Pearson product moment correlation coefficients were calculated between "trait" hostility and anxiety inventories and between these and the two measures of aggressive responses on the competitive reaction time task.

Results

Subjects
There were 16 subjects in each group: 14 males and 2 females and one subject in each group was nonwhite. The mean age (±SD) of forensic patients was 35.1 ± 12.0 years, range: 20–58. For the control patients the mean age was 40.7 ± 13.2 years, range: 21–63. The normal volunteer group had a mean age of 33.6 ± 11.4 years, range: 22–59. Patients were also matched for marital status, 11 living alone and 5 cohabiting in each group. With respect to education, all the forensic patients had left school by age 16, whereas half the control patients had some form of further education. Four of the forensic and 7 of the control patients were currently employed.

The healthy volunteers, recruited from a job centre, were all, of course, currently unemployed. Ten had left school by age 16, 15 were living alone and 6 were nonwhite. It was felt that this represented as feasible a match as possible with the two clinical samples.

Conviction questionnaire
The criminal profile of the groups was different ($F_{2,45}$ = 18.51; $P < 0.001$). As would be expected, forensic patients were involved in more acts of violence to people and property ($F_{1,45}$ = 7.63; $P < 0.01$), resulting in convictions.

Drinking questionnaire
The groups did not differ with respect to drinking. Group members drank three or four drinks on each occasion, on average once or twice a week. In the week before the test session each group consumed amounts similar to those in a usual week.

Buss–Durkee Hostility Inventory
The individual scales, the total score, and the motor aggression factor were analysed (see Table 4.3).

Assault.   This scale reflects physical violence against others and getting into fights. In this dimension the groups were significantly different, forensic patients admitting to more assaultive behaviour.

Indirect hostility.   This scale represents undirected hostility, such as temper tantrums, slamming doors, and throwing objects. No significant ($P < 0.05$) differences occurred between groups on this subscale but the forensic patients admitted to more indirect hostility than control patients.

TABLE 4.3
Buss–Durkee Hostility Inventory

Scales	Subjects			ANOVA					
	Forensic patients	Patient controls	Normal controls	Differences between groups		Normal vs. patients		Forensic vs. controls	
	Mean (SD)	Mean (SD)	Mean (SD)	$F_{2,45} =$	$P <$	$F_{1,45} =$	$P <$	$F_{1,45} =$	$P <$
Assault (0–10)	7.12 (1.7)	3.19 (1.6)	4.38 (2.9)	13.6	0.0001	n.s. .		25.85	0.0001
Indirect hostility (0–9)	6.08 (1.6)	4.56 (1.9)	5.00 (2.3)	2.6	0.09	n.s.		4.9	0.04
Verbal hostility (0–13)	8.41 (2.7)	6.25 (2.7)	8.62 (2.6)	3.75	0.04	n.s.		5.08	0.03
Irritability (0–11)	8.06 (1.6)	7.56 (1.8)	5.88 (3.0)	4.17	0.03	7.95	0.007	n.s.	
Negativism (0–5)	3.37 (1.5)	2.69 (1.4)	2.44 (1.3)		n.s.		n.s.	n.s.	
Resentment (0–8)	4.81 (1.9)	4.25 (1.9)	3.37 (2.4)		n.s.	3.25	0.08	n.s.	
Suspicion (0–10)	6.62 (2.0)	4.56 (2.3)	4.19 (2.6)	5.17	0.01	3.95	0.053	6.38	0.02
Guilt (0–9)	6.06 (1.8)	5.87 (2.4)	4.81 (2.1)		n.s.	3.16	0.09	n.s.	
Total (0–75)	50.55 (8.5)	38.94 (8.8)	38.69 (13.4)	6.69	0.03	3.56	0.07	9.82	0.003
Motor factor (0–43)	29.68 (5.9)	21.56 (5.5)	23.87 (8.4)	6.21	0.005	n.s.		11.69	0.02
STAS – Trait	25.87 (7.9)	23.62 (7.2)	24.31 (7.6)		n.s.	n.s.		n.s.	
STAS – State	12.37 (6.6)	14.87 (7.3)	12.50 (7.5)		n.s.	n.s.		n.s.	

Verbal hostility.   This scale represents behaviour such as shouting, arguing, and insulting other people. There was a significant difference between groups but this was accounted for by the patients. Healthy volunteers showed as much verbal hostility as forensic patients.

Irritability.   This scale involves feeling easily annoyed. In this case the difference between groups represented a difference between patients and normals. Both patient groups were more irritable.

Motor aggression factor.   Not surprisingly, this factor formed from the first listed four scales showed significant differences between groups. The forensic patients scored higher than the other groups.

Suspicion.   This scale reflects feelings that other people dislike you or are untrustworthy. There was a difference between groups. The forensic patients were more suspicious.

Negativism and *Resentment* showed no significant differences between groups, although forensic patients again had the highest scores (see Table 4.3).

Guilt.   Both groups of patients recorded more feelings of guilt than the healthy subjects but this result only approached statistical significance.

Total score.   The forensic patients obtained a much higher score than the other groups

Mood rating scale

Factor 1: alertness.   Eight of the nine scales loading on this factor showed significant differences, which were reflected in the factor score pre-task between the groups ($F_{2,45} = 7.25$; $P < 0.002$): normals were significantly more alert than patients ($F_{1,45} = 12.87$; $P < 0.001$) (see Fig. 4.1a). This difference between normals and patients ($F_{1,45} = 11.92$; $P < 0.002$) remained after the task.

Factor 2: contentment.   This factor was significant between the groups both pre-task ($F_{2,45} =10.06$; $P< 0.001$) when the normals were more content and over the experiment ($F_{2,45} = 10.79$; $P < 0.001$). Although contentment increased over time in all groups, patients remained less contented than the normals at both time points (see Fig. 4.1b). There was no difference between the two patient groups.

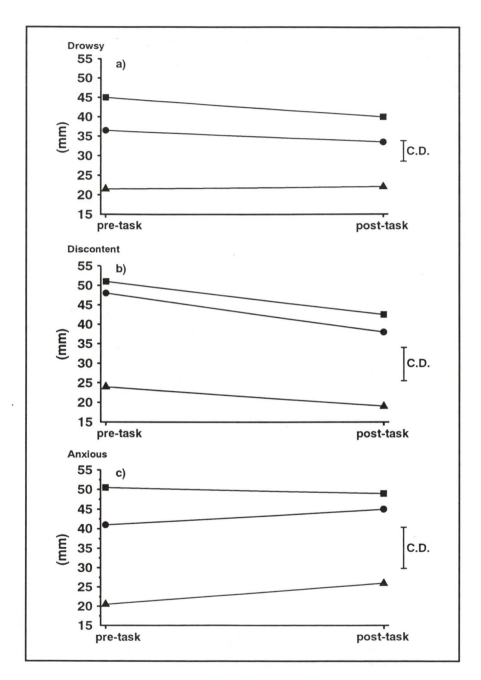

FIG. 4.1. Mean scores for the forensic patients (●), control patients (■), and healthy volunteers (▲) on (a) Factor 1 (alertness), (b) Factor 2 (contentment), and (c) Factor 3 (calmness) of the mood rating scale before and after the CRT. The $P < 0.05$ C.D. is displayed.

Factor 3: calmness.   This factor was significant between groups and between normals and patients both pre-task ($F_{2,45}$ = 9.0; P < 0.001) and overall ($F_{1,45}$ = 16.21; P < 0.001) (see Fig. 4.1c). Patients were less calm than normals, as expected, but there were no differences between the two patient groups.

Anger rating scale

Most of the 13 items on this scale were significantly different pre-task between groups and between normals and patients. Thus, both groups of patients were more hostile, angry, quarrelsome, etc. than normals. An example of one scale is depicted in Fig. 4.2. Time effects tended to differ between groups. Pre-task, patients felt more quarrelsome than normals, but post-task forensic patients tended to stay quarrelsome in contrast to the other groups ($F_{2,45}$ = 7.13; P < 0.01). Also in contrast to normals, both groups of patients became more resentful after the task ($F_{1,45}$ = 5.87; P < 0.02). In general, patients tended to be more angry than normals ($F_{1,45}$ = 17.88; P < 0.001), as shown on the mean scale score.

Spielberger State-Trait Anxiety Inventory

On the STAI-Trait the groups differed significantly ($F_{2,45}$ =14.71; P < 0.001), the two groups of patients being more anxious than the normals

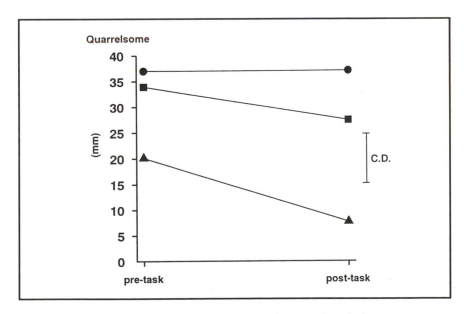

FIG. 4.2. Mean scores for the forensic patients (●), control patients (■), and healthy volunteers (▲) on VAS affable–quarrelsome from the ARS before and after the CRT.

($F_{1,45}$ = 26.82; P < 0.001) (see Fig. 4.3). The STAI-State showed significant differences pre-task between groups ($F_{2,45}$ = 14.21; P < 0.001), between normals and patients ($F_{1,45}$ = 22.07; P < 0.001), and between forensic and control patients ($F_{1,45}$ = 6.35; P < 0.02). Also the groups were significantly different overall ($F_{2,45}$ = 10.98; P < 0.001), as were normals compared with patients ($F_{1,45}$ = 18.94; P < 0.001). There were significant time effects within subject groups ($F_{1,45}$ = 9.81; P < 0.01): all subjects became slightly less anxious after the task.

Spielberger State-Trait Anger Scale
These scales failed to show any difference between groups either pre- or post-task. The pre-task means are shown in Table 4.3.

Physiological measures during simple reaction time task

EEG wavebands
The data were similar across all four wavebands. The power in the wavebands was significantly greater for the two patient groups than for the normal subjects (pre-task total power: $F_{1,44}$ = 6.8; P < 0.02) and this difference was maintained after the CRT (total power: $F_{1,44}$ = 7.17; P < 0.01). All groups dropped somewhat from pre-task to post-task ($F_{1,44}$

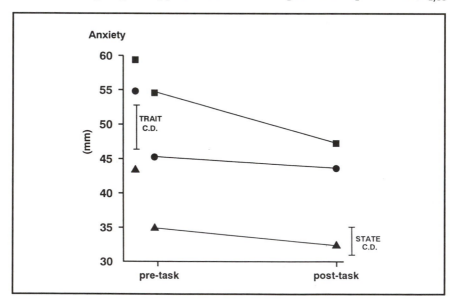

FIG. 4.3. Mean scores on the STAI-Trait (left) pre-testing and STAI-State before and after the CRT for the forensic patients (●), control patients (■), and healthy volunteers (▲).

= 8.07; $P < 0.01$) but these changes tended to be greater in the patient groups.

Auditory evoked potentials

Significant inter-group differences were found for the P_2 and N_2 latencies: the forensic group had shorter latencies than the control patients pre- but not post-task ($F_{1,45} = 5.91$; $P < 0.02$). No inter-group differences were found for the P_1 and N_1 latencies, nor for any of the evoked potential amplitudes.

Skin conductance level

The mean level did not differ between groups pre-task. However, the level dropped in the normal group but rose in the two patient groups, pre- to post-task, the interaction being significant ($F_{1,45} = 7.01$; $P < 0.02$).

Auditory reaction time

This speeded up from pre- to post-task, particularly in the normals ($F_{1,45} = 4.4$; $P < 0.05$).

Competitive reaction time task

Level set – Trial 1 (pre-provocation).   On the first trial, differences between groups on level set were not significant.

Trial blocks 1–3 (increasing provocation).   All subjects increased the level of noise set for their opponents through the task ($F_{2,44} = 4.6$; $P < 0.02$) with a linear trend ($F_{1,45} = 8.99$; $P < 0.01$) (see Fig. 4.4a). A significant difference was found between groups ($F_{2,45} = 3.24$; $P < 0.05$), and between forensic and control patients ($F_{1,45} = 5.99$; $P < 0.02$).

Duration set.   The duration of noise delivered to the opponent failed to show a significant difference between groups. However, the forensic patients tended to set longer noises overall.

Setting time.   No difference between groups was found on Trial 1. The time taken by all subjects to set the noise level decreased significantly through the blocks ($F_{2,44} = 4.55$; $P < 0.02$), with the forensic patients becoming quicker than control patients ($F_{2,44} = 3.53$; $P < 0.04$).

Reaction time.   No significant difference between groups on reaction time over all trials was found (see Fig. 4.4b). However, reaction times decreased over trials, particularly for forensic patients ($F_{2,44} = 15.27$; $P < 0.001$).

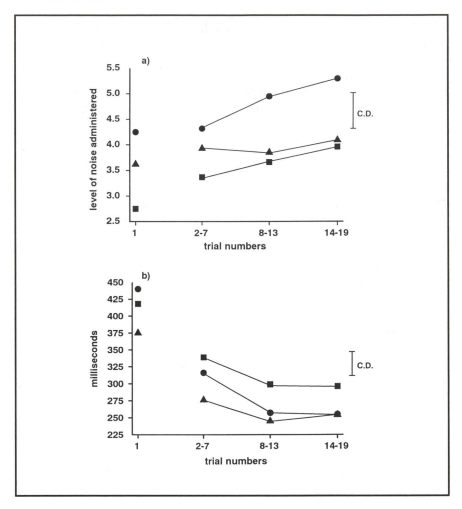

FIG. 4.4. Mean (a) levels of noise administered by the forensic (●),control (■), and healthy (▲) group to their opponent and (b) reaction time during each block of trials of the CRT.

Skin conductance and heart period

These two variables were measured throughout the competitive reaction time task, pre-trial, post-ready button pressed, etc. However, skin conductance showed no significant results.

Heart period.   *Trial 1.* The inter-beat interval (IBI) was measured at 6 points within the first trial (see Table 3.3). The mean heart period was different between normals and patients overall ($F_{1,44} = 3.73$; $P < 0.06$) (see Fig. 4.5). The normals had a longer heart period (i.e. slower heart rate). There was a significant difference between conditions within the trial ($F_{5,40} = 8.1$; $P < 0.001$), across groups, and a significant condition versus patients effect (see Table 4.4). The heart period had similarities between groups from the pre-trial to the middle of the block, but from post-amber light point (the warning signal) to the reaction time itself the pattern differed: The forensic patients shortened their heart period in a similar way to the normals but the control patients showed no change.

Trial blocks 1–3.   From trials 2 to 19 the heart period was examined over an additional event: post-win button (i.e. the duration of time subjects selected to deliver the noise to their opponent). The mean heart period did not change through the experiment but the significant difference between groups remained ($F_{2,44} = 4.2$; $P < 0.03$): The normals

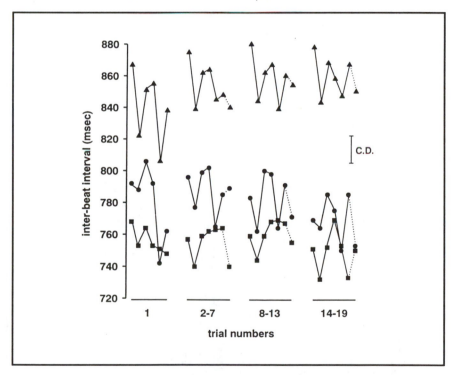

FIG. 4.5. The mean inter-beat interval of the heart rate pre-trial and after events within trial over successive blocks of trials for the forensic (●),control (■), and healthy (▲) groups. The individual points on each trial block represent pre-trial, post-ready, post-level displayed, post-amber light, post-RT and post-noise. The dotted line (....) represents when no noise was administered.

TABLE 4.4
Multivariate analyses of variance of heart period between events within trial between groups

Events within trial	Trial 1						Trials 2–19					
	Between groups			Forensic vs. control patients			Between groups			Forensic vs. control patients		
	df	F	P <	df	F	< P	df	F	P <	df	F	P <
Between events	10,80	2.42	0.02	5,40	3.55	0.02	12,78	2.42	0.01	6,39	2.63	0.03
Pre-trial vs. rest of trial		n.s.			n.s.		2,44	5.38	0.01		n.s.	
Post-volume display vs. post-ready button		n.s.			n.s.			n.s.			n.s.	
Post-amber vs. post-reaction time	2,44	3.76	0.03	1,44	5.71	0.02	2,44	4.27	0.02	1,44	8.51	0.005
Post-noise vs. events 2–5		n.s.			n.s.			n.s.			n.s.	
Events 2 & 3 vs. events 4 & 5	2,44	2.66	0.09	1,44	4.08	0.05	2,44	3.46	0.04	1,44	6.44	0.01
Noise vs. non-noise (linear)		—			—		2,44	4.84	0.02	1,44	9.27	0.004

had a longer heart period than patients ($F_{1,44}$ = 7.83; P < 0.01). There were significant effects (see Table 4.4) between conditions ($F_{6,39}$ = 10.62; P < 0.001) and between conditions versus groups across the experiment ($F_{12,78}$ = 2.43; P < 0.01) (see Fig. 4.5). There was a significant difference between pre-trial heart period and the rest of the trial: Normals showed more change than patients ($F_{1,44}$ = 10.55; P < 0.002). During trial events the control patients showed less change than on Trial 1, whereas the forensic patients were more like the normals. The forensic patients showed a lengthening in their heart period as the noise increased and a shortening when no noise occurred, whereas the control patients showed the opposite tendency.

Correlations between Trait Inventories

The total score of the Buss–Durkee Inventory correlated significantly with the Spielberger Trait Anger Scale (r = 0.49; P < 0.001). The subtotal of the four aggression scales, termed the motor component by Buss and Durkee (1957), also correlated significantly with the Trait Anger Scale (r = 0.53; P < 0.001). Both the total score of the Buss–Durkee and the Trait Anger Scale correlated with the Spielberger Trait Anxiety Inventory (r = 0.30; P < 0.05 and r = 0.39; P < 0.01, respectively).

Correlations between Trait Inventories and CRT behavioural aggression measures

The total score of the Buss–Durkee Hostility Inventory correlated significantly with the mean level of noise administered during the competitive reaction time task (r = 0.43; P < 0.01). The motor aggression factor and the individual Assault Scale also correlated with the level of noise administered (r = 0.32; P < 0.05; r = 0.40; P < 0.01, respectively). The Trait Anger Scale did not correlate significantly with this measure and neither questionnaire correlated significantly with the length of time for which the subjects administered the noise. The level of the noise set and the duration it was set for correlated weakly (r = 0.25; P < 0.10).

DISCUSSION

The main hypothesis was confirmed. The patients with a history of aggression responded with more behavioural aggression to provocation on the CRT than either the control patients or normal volunteers. We attempted to control as many individual variables as possible by matching the groups on demographic features so they had similar social status, and the three groups did not differ on drinking history nor on recent alcohol intake. However, there were differences in years of schooling. None of the forensic patients had any further education after the statutary school leaving age of 16. This may have been due to behavioural problems or interpersonal difficulties at school rather than intellectual ability. Nevertheless, we cannot rule out lower cognitive functioning as a contributory factor in their aggressive behaviour.

We attempted to match the two patient groups on primary diagnosis. However, far more of the forensic group had a second-level diagnosis of personality disorder. This is the most common diagnosis in patients displaying aggressive behaviour, but as pointed out in Chapter 1, the definition of antisocial personality disorder is circular in that a type of behaviour is used to define a disorder of personality. Therefore, the forensic patient's history of aggression would result in the diagnosis. Many authors have suggested that it is more helpful to look at dimensional measures (Kendell, 1982; Millon, 1981; van Praag et al., 1990) and so we used a range of these.

As might be expected, the patient groups differed from the healthy group on trait anxiety: Both showed levels of clinical anxiety (Spielberger et al., 1970) comparable to patients with anxiety disorders (Bruce & Lader, 1991). It has often been assumed that the relationship between anxiety and aggression is negative and that anxiety inhibits aggressive behaviour. However, a study that looked at the contribution of fear and anger to violence in forensic patients with delusional (paranoid) disorder found that all patients were rated positive on these two emotions both before and at the time of the offence (Kennedy, Kemp, & Dyer, 1992). The ratings were completed by both the patients and informants, and whereas patients more commonly described fears, informants described outbursts of anger. These patients then saw the world as a very threatening place and were responding to this. A group of violent offenders who rate highly on measures of anxiety and social inhibition has also been identified by Blackburn (1993). Anxiety may therefore represent a contributory factor to our patients' aggression. A similar pattern of anxiety was shown on the STAI-State, both patient groups showing significantly more anxiety than the healthy group. On this measure of current anxiety the control patients were significantly more anxious than the forensic group at initial testing but this diminished after the task, although both patient groups were still more anxious than normal controls.

There were major differences between groups on the questionnaire measures of aggression. Although not all the forensic patients had convictions, as a group they were more likely to have been involved in or convicted for acts of violence to people or property. This history was confirmed by their self-reports on the BDHI. The forensic patients admitted to exhibiting more physical violence, suspicion, and more aggression generally than the other groups who had similar scores to the original norms (Buss & Durkee, 1957). This confirms previous reports that have found prisoners convicted of violent crimes to score higher on the BDHI than those convicted of other crimes (Ehrenkranz, Bliss, & Sheard, 1974; Lothstein & Jones, 1978) and men who have committed domestic violence to score higher than nonviolent controls but no higher than generally violent men (Maiuro, Cahn, & Vitiliano, 1986; Maiuro, Cahn, Vitiliano, Wagner, & Zegree, 1988). This adds to the evidence for the concurrent validity of the BDHI. The forensic patients also differed from control patients on verbal hostility but not from the healthy volunteers. We do not know if this result would be replicated with another healthy group or if it was a characteristic of our healthy volunteer sample who were at the extreme on this dimension. Both groups of patients showed increased irritability relative to the healthy group. This does not support the postulation that irritability is related to overt aggressive acts, but the result may have been confounded by acts of attempted suicide or self-harm in both patient groups, irritability being related to aggression directed both outward and inward. Irritability may also be related to negative mood. There were no differences between groups on the anger scales, although there was a relationship between anger and both aggression and anxiety.

The patient groups were generally similar on current mood. They reported only average levels of alertness, contentment, calmness, and peacefulness on the visual analogue scales compared to healthy volunteers. This fits in with Beck's theory of negative self-evaluation by psychiatric patients (Beck, 1967) or indeed positive self-evaluation by normal subjects. The patients did not report extreme dysphoria, probably because they were receiving treatment. The differences in current mood between patients and healthy volunteers were maintained after the task but all subjects became more alert and excited, the forensic patients showing most change. All subjects also rated themselves as generally more contented and less hostile after the task. This may have been due to relief at the end of an aversive event (Mowrer, 1960). The changes on hostility were small and the forensic group showed no change, thus responding aggressively was not cathartic as would be predicted by frustration–aggression theory (Miller, 1941).

The patient groups also differed from the healthy volunteers on background psychophysiological measures. They exhibited higher power in all wavebands of the EEG pre-task. The fact that the patient groups were similar means this result is unlikely to be linked to aggression *per se*. A previous study has also shown higher cortical arousal in patients with anxiety disorders (Bond, James, & Lader, 1974) and so this finding may be linked to the high levels of trait anxiety shown by all the patients. Some work has linked antisocial, criminal behaviour to underarousal on both central and peripheral psychophysiological measures (Raine, Venables, & Williams, 1990). Although this work examined serious offending such as recorded in the Criminal Records Office, it was not confined to aggressive acts and this may be one reason why conflicting results have been obtained (Mednick, Pollock, Volavka, & Gabrielli, 1982). Blackburn (1993) has identified two separate groups of violent offenders, one with high anxiety and one without, and so our patients may be similar to the former group. Their aggressive behaviour may be due to their perception of the world as a threatening place and their impulsive response to perceived provocation. Studies of social expectations have confirmed this. The secondary psychopathic group identified by Blackburn (1993) expected other people to challenge them, i.e. to argue, wind you up, be sarcastic, and not to be friendly or attentive. There was a tendency for slow-wave activity to decrease and fast-wave activity to increase post-task and these changes were most apparent in the patient groups on fast-wave activity, increasing their differences from normal. This may indicate more psychophysiological response to a stressful situation in people with psychological problems than is shown in healthy controls. Some confirmation of this interpretation is given by the skin conductance level results. The control patients showed slightly lower levels pre-task but both patient groups increased their levels post-task, whereas the normal subjects decreased, i.e. became more relaxed. The increased arousal of the patient groups may also have interfered with simple reaction time performance. There were no differences between groups pre-task but the normal controls improved their performance more and were therefore significantly faster than the control patients post-task.

Our major behavioural measure of aggression was the volume of noise the subjects set for their "opponent". The forensic patients set higher levels of noise throughout the task but this was not significant before provocation was introduced. With increasing levels of provocation, all subjects tended to increase the volume of noise they set but this was significantly greater for the forensic group. The forensic group also administered longer periods of noise to their opponent but this measure did not reach statistical significance. Although the duration of noise administered might be considered a more direct form of aggressive behaviour, it did not involve provocation in this experiment as the durations of noise administered to the subjects varied randomly and did not increase. The fact that patients with a history of aggression respond more aggressively on the CRT task gives external validity to the task. The CRT is able to identify subjects who are likely to respond aggressively to perceived provocation in the world outside the laboratory. The time taken to choose a level of noise to be administered to the opponent decreased through the task for all subjects. The healthy group were fastest but both the forensic and the healthy groups were more decisive than the control patients.

Heart period and skin conductance level were monitored throughout the task. The heart period was consistently shorter in the patient groups, confirming the increased arousal shown on the other psychophysiological measures. The healthy subjects also showed greater recovery between trials, i.e. their heart rate returned to its resting level before each trial, whereas the patient groups showed no recovery. Within trial the forensic group showed similar changes to the healthy subjects, whereas the control patients were less reactive to events. Both normal and forensic groups showed an increase in heart period in response to hearing the noise and a decrease when they administered it to their opponent, whereas the control patients tended to show the opposite. Any differences therefore do not seem to be due to aggression, although there was an indication that the forensic group were more reactive within trial as well as showing less recovery between trials.

The major finding in this experiment is that forensic patients behave more aggressively on a laboratory task of aggression, the CRT. We also found a correlation between self-reported aggressive behaviour on the BDHI and behavioural aggression on the task. Thus, there was a relationship between a history of aggressive acts, a trait of aggressiveness, and behaviour on a laboratory task. This gives external validity to this laboratory task, which can induce aggressive behaviour in a similar way to that found previously by other authors using shocks (Taylor, 1967). It should therefore be a good method of measuring aggression induced by drugs.

SUMMARY

Sixteen patients with a history of aggression, 16 control patients and 16 healthy volunteers, all matched for demographic features, took part in the study. They competed on a competitive reaction time task and filled in self-ratings both before and after the task. Some psychophysiological measures were recorded before and after the task and cardiac and electrodermal activity were monitored during it. Both groups of patients differed from healthy subjects on self-ratings of mood and background psychophysiology. They rated themselves as less alert and more discontent, anxious, and irritable, and they showed higher voltage levels on the EEG. The patient groups diverged on the measures of aggression. The forensic patients showed more behavioural aggression on the task than both the other groups, especially at high levels of provocation. They also rated themselves as more aggressive on the BDHI and these two measures correlated. The CRT therefore proved to be a valid measure of aggression.

CHAPTER FIVE

The effects of alcohol on behavioural aggression

INTRODUCTION

Because of its association with both violent and nonviolent crime (Murdoch, Pihl, & Ross, 1990; Smith & Burvill, 1987), alcohol is generally believed to facilitate aggression. Laboratory studies have shown that alcohol increases aggressive behaviour under conditions of provocation (Gustafson, 1993) and interpersonal threat (Gantner & Taylor, 1992). Various explanations have been postulated for the effects of alcohol on aggression. Expectancy effects are powerful (Lang, Goeckner, Adesso, & Marlatt, 1975) and although alcohol is usually consumed to induce powerful positive feelings such as euphoria, anxiety reduction, and social disinhibition (Zuckerman, 1987), heavy social drinkers also expect it to increase their aggression (Rohsenow & Bachorowski, 1984). Male drinkers in particular consume alcohol to enhance feelings of power and strength (McClelland, Davis, Kalin, & Wanner, 1972) and this may legitimise acts of aggression (Collins, 1981).

Alcohol is also known to increase physiological arousal and it has been suggested that this state might strengthen aggressive tendencies (Boyatzis 1983). Although alcohol has indeed been shown to raise basal levels of heart rate and skin conductance (Cohen, Schandler, & Naliboff, 1983; Dengerink & Fagan, 1978; Levenson, Sher, Grossman, Newman,

& Newlin, 1980), it has also been shown to decrease reactivity to stress (Levenson et al., 1980; Sher & Levenson, 1982). This so-called "stress response dampening" is predicted to occur when an unequivocal stressor is used, and a higher dose (over 1g/kg) of alcohol given. It has been seen when anxiety has been induced in stress tasks (Levenson et al., 1980; Sher & Levenson, 1982) but has not been examined in a task evoking anger or aggression. We decided, therefore, to quantify the effects of two doses of alcohol, low (0.25g/kg) and moderate (0.75g/kg), on the behaviour induced by the competitive reaction time task and on cardiac and electrodermal activity during the task.

Methods

Subjects
Subjects were recruited via advertisements posted on the institutional notice-board and by personal communication, and were paid for participating in a single session. Forty-five subjects took part in the study, 24 females and 21 males, divided into 3 groups, each with 8 females and 7 males. The first group had a mean age of 28.5 years and a mean weight of 68.7kg, the second group 26.6 years and 65.8kg and the third group 26.4 years and 68.3kg.

Drugs and procedure
The study was approved by the appropriate Ethical Committee and each subject gave informed consent. Two doses of alcohol (as vodka) and a placebo were used. Group 1 received the moderate dose, 0.75g/kg alcohol for males. The Widmark factor was used to calculate the dose for females: They received 83% of the male dose so as to achieve the same breath alcohol concentration. The mean amount of vodka given was 164.4ml (198.2 for males; 134.8 for females) made up to 250ml with low-calorie tonic and flavoured with 5ml lime juice. Group 2 received the low dose, 0.25g/kg alcohol, so that the mean volume of vodka given was 53.2ml (62.8 for males; 44.7 for females) made up to 250ml with low-calorie tonic and 5 ml lime juice. Group 3 received 240ml low calorie tonic with 5ml lime juice and 5ml of vodka was floated on the top of the drink to try to maintain the double-blind. Subjects were allowed 15 minutes to consume their drink. They were instructed not to drink any alcohol for 24 hours before testing and not to eat or drink anything (except water) after midnight on the test morning. They completed the first set of measures before the drink at 9.30 a.m. The competitive reaction time task was run 1 hour after the drink had been consumed.

Measures

Breath alcohol concentration
A Lion (Cardiff, UK) Alcolmeter AE-M2 was used to estimate breath alcohol concentrations. The subject inhaled, then blew into the mouthpiece continuously for 6 seconds and the expiration was sampled at 4 seconds. The breath alcohol concentration was measured pre-drink and at 30-minute intervals for 2 hours after the drink. A new mouthpiece was used for each sample.

Competitive reaction time task
This was presented as detailed in Chapter 3. Heart period and skin conductance were recorded during the task as set out in Chapter 3.

Subjective rating scales
The Mood Rating Scale, Anger Rating Scale, and Spielberger State Anxiety Inventory (see Chapter 3) were completed pre-drink, 1 hour post-drink before the competitive reaction time task and immediately after it. The Drinking Questionnaire was filled in once, pre-drink.

Guess concerning alcohol
Subjects were asked to estimate the amount of alcohol they had consumed on a five-point scale from nil to very large. This was completed 1 hour after the drink.

Analysis of data
Multivariate analysis of variance between groups, time, sex, and the interactions thereof was used to analyse the data both for the variables measured pre- and post-task and for the variables measured on the four blocks of trials of the task. Patterns of trends over time were also examined and contrast analysis was used to evaluate differences in treatments. A least significant difference (LSD) *t*-test was used to compare means within a significant ANOVA. A repeated measured multivariate analysis of variance with a between-subjects model of sex and groups and a within-subjects model of event and time was used to analyse the heart period. A priori contrasts were selected.

Results

Breath alcohol concentration
No alcohol was detected on the placebo occasion. On the low dose occasions, concentrations ranged from 36.3mg/100ml 30 minutes after

ingestion to 12.5mg/100ml at 90 minutes. The corresponding figures for the higher dose occasion were 99.9 and 79.1mg/100ml, respectively.

Guess concerning alcohol

The placebo and higher dose groups differed in their detection of alcohol but the difference between placebo and low-dose groups was not significant.

Competitive reaction time task

Level set – Trial 1 (pre-provocation). The dosage groups differed significantly on Trial 1 ($F_{2,39} = 4.09$; $P < 0.03$) (see Fig 5.1). The alcohol groups set higher levels, although this was confined to the higher dose in females.

Trial blocks 1–4. The noise levels increased with blocks of trials for all groups ($F_{3,40} = 11.39$; $P < 0.001$). The dosage groups differed significantly ($F_{2,42} = 5.81$; $P < 0.006$), the higher alcohol group in particular

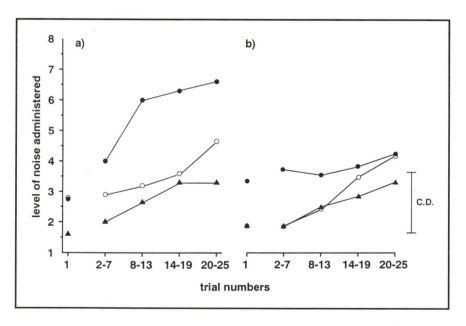

FIG. 5.1. Mean levels of noise administered by (a) male and (b) female subjects after a moderate dose of alcohol (●), a low dose of alcohol (○), and placebo (▲). The 0.05 critical difference applies to the blocks of trials.

setting higher levels. However, differences were seen between the sexes, males increasing their settings more than females ($F_{6,74} = 2.76$; $P < 0.02$) (see Fig. 5.1).

Setting time. No significant differences between groups were found.

Reaction time. All subjects decreased their RT through the task ($F_{3,40} = 6.37$; $P < 0.001$). There was a significant difference between groups ($F_{2,42} = 3.81$; $P < 0.03$), subjects on the higher dose of alcohol were slightly slower and those on the low dose were slightly faster than subjects on placebo. The difference was therefore significant between doses ($F_{1,42} = 7.65$; $P < 0.01$).

Physiological measures

Skin conductance level and fluctuations

The skin conductance level (SCL) tended to increase throughout the experiment (increased arousal). The SCL also rose during each trial and this rise increased as the trials progressed ($F_{3,40} = 4.76$; $P < 0.007$). No intergroup differences were found. The number of fluctuations increased from pre-trial to the rest of the trial ($F_{3,37} = 31.4$; $P < 0.001$) and after the noise compared to no-noise ($F_{3,37} = 16.3$; $P < 0.001$) irrespective of group.

Heart period

Trial 1. The heart period (inter-beat interval) shortened from immediately before the start of the trial to subsequent points within the trial. After the subject set the level of noise, the heart temporarily slowed. There were no significant interactions with alcohol.

Trial blocks 1–4. The heart period shortened over time for all groups, i.e. the heart rate rose. During the trial the pattern was similar to that in Trial 1. The exception was the change from after the warning signal to after the response (RT), which showed an interaction with groups. The higher alcohol group showed a tachycardia, whereas the other two groups slowed down ($F_{2,39} = 5.71$; $P < 0.007$). All groups showed a shorter heart period after the noise.

Overall, placebo and alcohol groups showed differences. The alcohol groups had raised heart rates ($F_{1,39} = 4.07$; $P < 0.05$) and less change within trials ($F_{2,39} = 4.5$; $P < 0.05$) (see Fig. 5.2).

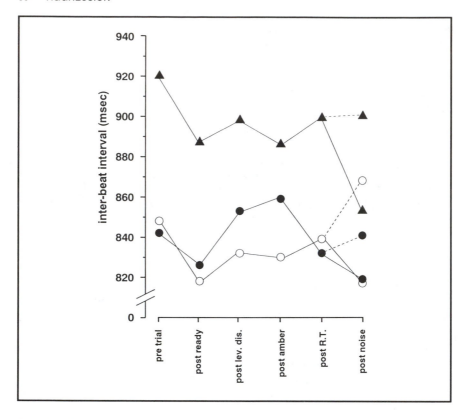

FIG. 5.2. The mean inter-beat interval of the heart rate pre-trial and after events within trial for trials 2–25 after a moderate dose of alcohol (●), a low dose of alcohol (○), and placebo (▲). The dashed line (- - -) represents when no noise was administered.

Subjective rating scales

Drinking questionnaire
The groups did not differ with respect to drinking behaviour. Overall subjects drank once or twice a week or at weekends only and consumed three or four drinks on each occasion.

Mood rating scale

Factor 1: alertness.   There was an overall difference between groups on this factor ($F_{2,42} = 4.12$; $P < 0.03$). The higher dose of alcohol made subjects feel generally drowsier. Most of the scale items on this factor also showed a significant time effect, the subjects finding the task "alerting", which was reflected in the factor score ($F_{1,42}$ =17.80; $P < 0.001$). There was no interaction between groups and time.

Factor 2: contentment.   Subjects in all groups became less contented after the task ($F_{1,42} = 11.12$; $P < 0.01$).

Factor 3: calmness.   All groups became more calm and relaxed after the drink but this effect was reversed by the task ($F_{1,42} = 95.27$; $P < 0.001$). The three groups had similar pre-task values but the placebo group showed more change than the alcohol groups after the task (see Fig. 5.3a), becoming significantly more anxious ($F_{2,42} = 3.32$; $P < 0.05$).

Anger rating scale
Subjects in all groups became more angry and hostile after the task ($F_{1,42}$ = 16.21; $P < 0.001$). Alcohol tended to attenuate this effect, e.g. furious–calm ($F_{1,42} = 6.04$; $P < 0.02$) (see Fig. 5.3b).

Spielberger State Anxiety Inventory
This showed a significant time effect, all subjects irrespective of group becoming more anxious after the task ($F_{1,42}$ = 37.76; $P < 0.001$). The placebo group showed most anxiety.

DISCUSSION

The competitive reaction time task was run at a time when breath alcohol levels were maximal and beginning to decrease, as this is when adverse mood effects are most likely to occur (Myrsten, 1971). The placebo control double-blind was successful in that subjects in the placebo group believed that they had received a dose of alcohol indistinguishable from the low dose. However, subjects in the moderate dose group, with breath alcohol concentration averaging 0.1 per cent, did rate themselves as receiving more than either of the other two groups and presumably recognised the intoxicating effects of alcohol.

Emotional and behavioural aggression was elicited by the competitive reaction time task in all groups. The measure of behavioural aggression was taken as the level of noise the subjects set for their opponent. Subjects in the higher alcohol group set this level higher to start with and continued to set significantly higher levels than the placebo group. The male and female subjects in the placebo and low dose groups behaved in a similar way. However, in the moderate dose group, although both male and female subjects started off more aggressively, they then diverged. The males increased their settings steeply, whereas

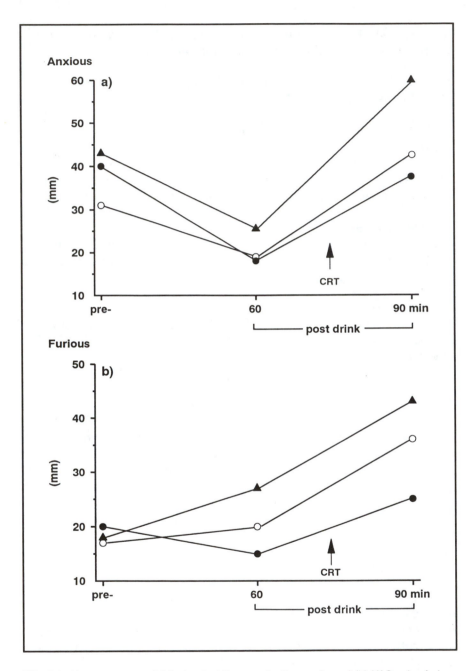

FIG. 5.3. Mean scores on (a) factor 3 of the mood rating scale and (b) VAS calm–furious pre-drink, post-drink, and post-task after a moderate dose of alcohol (●), a low dose(○), or placebo (▲).

the females increased them very little. This difference was not reflected in any other measure but there is evidence that although women experience as much anger as men, they respond with less physical aggression (Frost & Averill, 1982; Gustafson, 1986).

The major physiological effect was an increase in activity as the trials proceeded. The heart period shortened as the noise settings rose. A specific pattern within each trial was discernable. Thus, the heart period shortened from the resting condition to events within trial and from these to the noise. Effects of a novel noise stimulus have been shown to be substantial (Turpin & Siddle, 1983) and the noise condition in this experiment kept the heart rate elevated compared to when no noise occurred. The heart period consistently lengthened at one point in the trial, while the subjects waited to see a light display of the noise they would receive at the end of the trial, should they "lose". This change was in the predicted direction for anticipation (Obrist, 1982) and was not altered by alcohol.

Nevertheless, distinct cardiac effects were induced by alcohol. It increased basal cardiac activity but suppressed reactivity to events within the trial. This supports the hypothesis that alcohol exerts a stress-response dampening effect on cardiac activity at the point of stress (Levenson et al., 1980). As not only cardiac responsivity to stress (Eves & Gruzelier, 1984; Light & Obrist, 1983) but also the stress-response dampening (SRD) effect of alcohol (Sher & Levenson, 1983) differs in individuals, these effects must have been strong to show up in a nonselected group. It is also possible that the CRT by inducing anger and aggression as well as anxiety created more stress than the previous tasks employed.

The only sex difference found on the physiological measures was that females had lower skin conductance levels than males, which replicates a previous finding (Bond & Lader, 1986). Electrodermal activity increased overall in a way similar to cardiac functioning, but the change within trial was more marked than that across trials. Subjects seeemed able to recover between trials with respect to skin conductance level, but then all groups showed a marked response to events within the trial and to increasing levels of noise. Alcohol did not show an SRD effect on electrodermal activity. A dissociation was therefore found between heart rate and electrodermal activity, but not in the direction predicted from Gray's (1975) theory (Fowles, 1980).

Mood was clearly altered by the competitive task. Subjects in all groups became more alert, less contented, and more anxious. Alcohol had some calming effect and also tended to lessen feelings of hostility. These effects are consistent with the tension-reducing hypothesis (Conger, 1956; Kraft, 1971), but this still does not account for the increased behavioural aggression induced by alcohol. Response disinhibition seems unlikely as the increase in behavioural aggression is linked to the increasing provocation of the "opponent". The SRD effect of alcohol may result from an influence on a cognitive process altering the evaluation of a level of threat (Levenson et al., 1980). Hull (1981) provides a model of self-awareness linked to this that states that "alcohol does not serve to reduce tension directly but rather serves to reduce cognisance of a potential source of tension". Alcohol would therefore be consumed to reduce self-awareness and the consumption would decrease the individual's responsiveness to situational norms of appropriate behaviour. Some support for Hull's theory comes from studies in which subjects who had consumed alcohol behaved more aggressively to opponents irrespective of behavioural contingencies (Cherek, Steinberg, & Manno, 1985; Gustafson, 1985; Zeichner & Pihl, 1979, 1980). The theory would also account for our finding of increased aggressive behaviour after alcohol even prior to any provocation and without the same levels of tension, anxiety, or anger felt by the placebo group. Another theory that has developed out of experimental work on alcohol and aggression (Taylor & Leonard, 1983) suggests that alcohol impairs attentional capacity so that attention is only directed to the most salient external cues. In this experiment the provocation of receiving increasing levels of noise would be the most salient contextual cue. Studies that have introduced cues leading to self-awareness have shown that alcohol-instigated aggression can be reduced (Bailey, Leonard, Cranston, & Taylor, 1983; Jeavons & Tayler, 1985).

SUMMARY

Alcohol in two doses (0.75g/kg and 0.25g/kg) and a placebo were administered to three matched groups of subjects. After one hour, the subjects took part in a competitive reaction time task during which they both experienced and had the opportunity to administer increasing noise levels. Cardiac and electrodermal activity were monitored throughout and subjects completed ratings of mood, anger, and anxiety pre- and post-drink and post-task. It was found that as the noise level they received increased, subjects in all groups displayed higher cardiac and electrodermal responsiveness. Alcohol increased behavioural aggression without a concomitant increase in any of the mood states measured, and showed a stress-response dampening effect on cardiac but not electrodermal activity.

CHAPTER SIX

The effects of benzodiazepines on behavioural aggression

INTRODUCTION

Benzodiazepines have been in clinical use since the early 1960s. Initially they were claimed to have anti-aggressive as well as anxiolytic properties, although the animal literature has been equivocal (Rodgers & Waters, 1985), differing according to species and test. Reports of rage attacks in humans occurred early on (e.g. Boyle & Tobin, 1961) and were labelled paradoxical reactions as they tended to occur in isolated instances and usually at high doses (Bond & Lader, 1979). Reports have continued with the newer benzodiazepines (Rosenbaum et al., 1984). Laboratory studies have suggested that chlordiazepoxide and diazepam but not oxazepam increase hostility or aggressive responding (Gardos et al., 1968; Salzman et al., 1974, 1975; Wilkinson, 1985).

It is thus possible that benzodiazepines differ in their propensity to release aggressive behaviour. Increasing awareness of problems with the benzodiazepines, e.g. dependence and amnesic episodes, has led to attempts to differentiate among them. Duration of action has been used as one attribute, short-acting compounds being assumed not to accumulate, although offset of effect may be disconcertingly abrupt (e.g. rebound insomnia). However, other parameters have also been suggested as relevant, for example, potency and ceiling efficacy. The former refers to the dosage required for a criterion effect, the latter to the maximum effect irrespective of dosage.

One way to investigate these putative differential effects is to compare two compounds of similar pharmacokinetic properties at comparable doses (to obviate potency differences) to see whether the profile of activity differs. If it does, and potency differences really have been taken out of the equation, then the results probably reflect genuine efficacy differences. This in turn has implications for hypotheses concerning the mode of action of the drugs at the receptor level and also for the development of newer benzodiazepine-like drugs with improved risk/benefit ratios.

Two intermediate-acting benzodiazepines that have both been used extensively to control daytime anxiety are lorazepam and oxazepam (Greenblatt, Shader, Divoll, & Harmatz, 1981). They differ in structure by only one chlorine atom but they have different clinical potencies, lorazepam being 15 times more potent than oxazepam. Also, ceiling efficacies seem different, lorazepam being much more likely to impair memory functions at an equivalent clinical dose (Curran, Schiwy, & Lader, 1987). As oxazepam has not been implicated in either rage attacks or hostility engendered in a laboratory paradigm, it seemed an ideal comparison for the more potent lorazepam in our competitive reaction time task. The two drugs were used in doses that were considered, according to the official Data Sheets, to be equipotent in the clinical control of anxiety.

Methods

Subjects
Subjects were recruited via advertisements posted on the institutional notice-board. They were paid for participating. Forty-five normal healthy volunteers took part in the study, 20 females and 25 males. Their age range was 19–46 years with a mean age of 26 years. They were divided into five groups, each with 4 females and 5 males.

Drugs and procedure
The study was approved by the appropriate Ethical Committee and written informed consent was obtained from all subjects. A double-blind independent five-group design was used to compare the treatments: oxazepam 15 and 30mg, lorazepam 1 and 2mg, and placebo. Subjects were instructed not to take any alcohol or other CNS drugs for 24 hours before testing and not to take substances containing caffeine on the test day. The ratings were completed before and 4 hours after drug

administration and after the competitive reaction time task (4.5 hours post-drug). The competitive reaction time task was run starting 4 hours post-drug.

Measures

Competitive reaction time task
This was run as detailed in Chapter 3. Physiological measures were also recorded during the task, again as described in Chapter 3.

Subjective rating scales
The Mood Rating Scale, Anger Rating Scale and Spielberger State-Trait Anxiety Inventory were administered as set out in Chapter 3.

Analysis of data
Multivariate analysis (between groups, time, sex, and the interactions thereof) was used to analyse data both for the ratings, which were measured three times, and for the variables measured on the four blocks of trials of the CRT task. Patterns of trends over time were examined and contrast analysis was used to evaluate differences in treatments with the following planned pair-wise comparisons: placebo versus active drugs; oxazepam versus lorazepam; high doses versus low doses.

Results

Competitive reaction time task

Level set – Trial 1 (nonprovocation).   The drug groups did not differ on Trial 1. Males in all groups set higher levels than females ($F_{1,33} = 4.48$; $P < 0.05$).

Trial blocks 1–4 (increasing provocation).   Males continued to set higher noise levels than females overall ($F_{1,33} = 4.58$; $P < 0.04$) and subjects on active treatment set higher levels than those on placebo ($F_{4,33} = 3.52$; $P < 0.02$) (see Fig. 6.1). All groups set higher levels with increasing provocation ($F_{3,31} = 31.24$; $P < 0.001$ but the groups differed with respect to the size of this increase ($F_{12,82} = 2.15$; $P < 0.03$) (see Fig. 6.1). Levels were significantly higher in the high dose lorazepam than the high dose oxazepam group ($F_{1,33} = 5.08$; $P < 0.04$). An interaction occurred between high and low doses and time ($F_{3,31} = 3.35$; $P < 0.04$): The high dose of lorazepam showed most increase. There were no drug effects on setting time or reaction time.

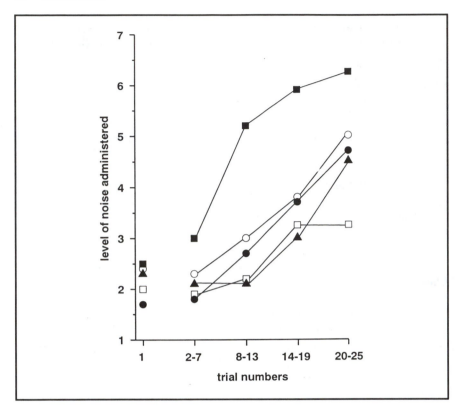

FIG. 6.1. Mean levels of noise administered by subjects after lorazepam 1mg (□), 2mg (■) oxazepam 15mg (○), 30mg (●), and placebo (▲) during each block of trials of the CRT.

Physiological measures

Skin conductance level and fluctuation

Trial 1. There were no significant differences between groups on the basal level of skin conductance, the change within trial, or the number of fluctuations on trial one. Fluctuations increased from pre-trial to during the trial ($F_{1,37} = 38.43$; $P < 0.001$).

Trial blocks 1–4. All subjects showed an increase in baseline skin conductance level through the experiment ($F_{3,30} = 40.59$; $P < 0.001$). There was no difference between drugs. The change in level within each trial also showed an increase through the experiment ($F_{3,30} = 6.98$; $P < 0.01$) but the drugs × times interaction also showed a significant quadratic trend ($F_{4,32} = 3.23$; $P < 0.05$). The subjects on oxazepam showed more change within trial as the experiment progressed. The number of fluctuations increased through the experiment ($F_{3,35}$ = 4.31; $P < 0.01$) and showed a highly significant difference within trial between conditions ($F_{3,35}$ = 81.67; $P < 0.001$). Fluctuations increased from pre-trial to the rest of the trial and from during the trial to after the RT and there were more fluctuations after the noise than when no noise occurred. There was a significant interaction between condition and drug ($F_{12,92}$ = 1.95; $P < 0.05$). Subjects on oxazepam showed a greater increase in fluctuations from during the trial to after the reaction time (see Fig. 6.2).

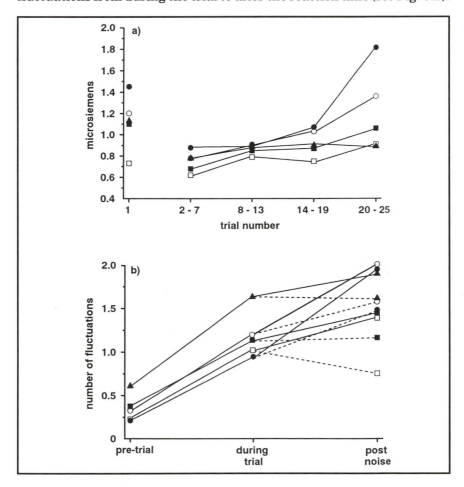

FIG. 6.2. Mean (a) skin conductance levels during each block of trials and (b) number of fluctuations within trial. The dashed line (- - -) represents when no noise was administered. Values shown after lorazepam 1mg (□), 2mg (■), oxazepam 15mg (○), 30mg (●), and placebo (▲).

Heart period

Trial 1.   The heart period showed a similar pattern of effects (see Table 6.1) as found previously (Chapter 5). It shortened from immediately before the start of the trial to subsequent points within the trial and from after the warning signal for the reaction time (RT) to after the RT itself. The drugs did not alter this pattern but there was a drug × type interaction on the change from resting level to events within trial ($F_{4,31} = 4.57$; $P < 0.01$). The high dose of oxazepam group showed a greater change than the other groups.

Trial blocks 1–4.   The heart period again showed a distinct pattern of effects (see Table 6.1). It shortened from pre-trial to events within trial, from no noise to noise condition, and it lengthened from after the subjects had set the noise level to be delivered to their opponent to after the display of the level they themselves would receive. This pattern was not affected by the drugs. There was an overall significant difference between drugs because subjects on both doses of oxazepam had a longer heart period than those on placebo or lorazepam ($F_{4,31} = 5.71$; $P < 0.01$). There was also a significant effect across trial blocks ($F_{3,29} = 4.13$; $P < 0.05$). The heart period initially became longer but then shortened through the experiment. There was no significant interaction with the pattern within trial.

Subjective rating scales

Mood rating scale

Factor: 1 alertness.   All subjects became more drowsy 4 hours after drug administration ($F_{1,33} = 14.73$; $P < 0.001$) and then more alert after the task ($F_{1,33} = 74.52$; $P < 0.001$) (see Fig. 6.3a). The subjects on active treatment became more drowsy than those on placebo ($F_{1,33} = 3.03$; $P < 0.05$) but there was no difference between groups post-task.

Factor 2: contentment.   There were no drug effects on this factor but the females in all groups were more discontented than the males, both before and after tablet administration and the task.

Factor 3: calmness.   The subjects in all groups tended to become calmer post-tablet administration ($F_{1,33} = 4.07$; $P < 0.06$) and more tense post-task ($F_{1,33} = 24.66$; $P < 0.001$) (see Fig. 6.3b). There were no drug effects.

TABLE 6.1
Multivariate analysis of variance of heart period between events within trial with a priori contrasts

	Trial 1				*Trials 2–25*		
Events within trial	*df*	*F*	*P*	*Events within trial*	*df*	*F*	*P*
Between events	5,27	5.27	0.002	Between events	6,26	22.95	0.0001
A priori contrasts				*A priori contrasts*			
Pre-trial vs. rest of trial	1,31	23.6	0.0001	Pre-trial vs. rest of trial	1,31	20.24	0.0001
Post-ready button vs. post-level display	1,31	0.85		Post-ready button vs. post-level display	1,31	73.75	0.0001
Post-amber light vs. post-RT	1,31	14.8	0.0006	Post-amber light vs. post-RT	1,31	0.89	
Events 2–5 vs. post-noise	1,31	0.26		Post-noise vs. post -no noise	1,31	35.79	0.0001
Events 2 + 3 vs. events 4 + 5	1,31	13.62	0.0009				

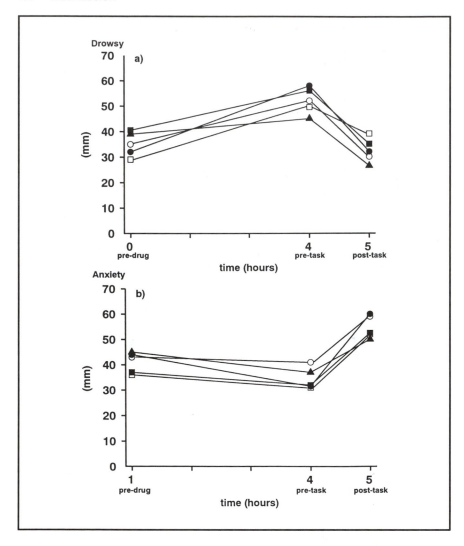

FIG. 6.3. Mean scores on (a) Factor 1 (alertness) and (b) Factor 3 (calmness) of the mood rating scale.Values shown after lorazepam 1mg (□), 2mg (■), oxazepam 15mg (○), 30mg (●), and placebo (▲).

Anger rating scale
Twelve of the 13 items of the ARS showed significant effects over time. The subjects rated themselves as more peaceful post-drug (10 items) and more angry post-task (12 items) (see Fig. 6.4). Only one item (belligerent–restrained) also showed an interaction between drugs and

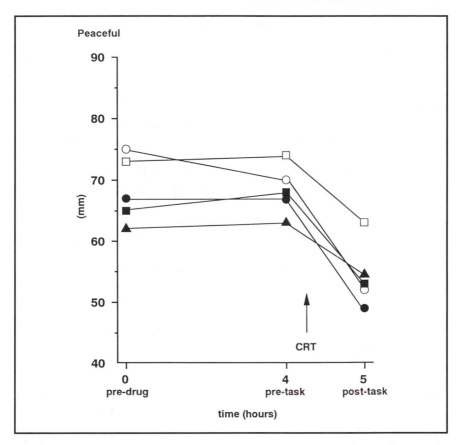

FIG. 6.4. Mean scores on VAS angry–peaceful pre-drug, 4 hours post-drug and post-CRT. Values shown after lorazepam 1mg (□), 2mg (■), oxazepam 15mg (○), 30mg (●), and placebo (▲).

time ($F_{4,33} = 3.38$; $P < 0.02$) and a difference between high and low doses on this interaction ($F_{1,33} = 9.16$; $P < 0.01$). Subjects on the high doses of lorazepam and oxazepam rated themselves as significantly more belligerent after the task than before it.

Spielberger State-Trait Anxiety Inventory
There were no significant differences between groups on the STAI-Trait, administered before the experiment. The mean score was 37.7. There were no significant differences between groups on the STAI-State. Subjects in all groups became more anxious after the task ($F_{1,33} = 8.87$; $P < 0.01$).

DISCUSSION

Lorazepam and oxazepam are very similar in structure and pharmacology and might therefore be expected to have a similar profile of effects in the tests we used. This was so for the subjective measures: Some sedation was shown after both drugs but neither showed anxiolytic effects compared with placebo. However, the two drugs diverged with respect to their effects on the competitive reaction time task. Although initially the same, the groups became differentiated as the trials progressed. All groups increased the volume of the noise they intended to administer to their "opponent" but the high dose lorazepam group selected the highest noise levels. Nevertheless, the groups generally did not differ in their self-ratings of anger or hostility. The doses of each drug used were believed to be equipotent in clinical terms and produced comparable levels of sedation. The lower dose levels of the drugs were indistinguishable, and they only diverged at the higher dose. This raises the question as to whether even higher dose levels of oxazepam would have induced hostility comparable to that of the 2mg dose of lorazepam. However, excessive drowsiness would probably preclude testing.

Could the differential effect merely reflect potency as a factor rather than ceiling efficacy? Lorazepam is 15 times more potent than oxazepam. Potency is generally regarded as unimportant for clinical purposes (Gilman, Mayer, & Melmon, 1980) but it may have some relevance for adverse effects. More problems are generally encountered in withdrawing patients from benzodiazepines with short elimination half-lives and high potency (Martinez-Cano, Vela-Bueno, de Iceta, Pomalima, & Martinez-Gras, 1995; Tyrer, Rutherford, & Huggett, 1981). Alternatively, the difference may be related to ceiling efficacy, and lorazepam may exert a maximal effect on such behaviour at a lower equivalent dose than oxazepam. Disproportional effects of this dose of lorazepam have also been displayed on memory functions (Curran et al., 1987). Comparisons between diazepam, oxazepam, and lorazepam found only lorazepam to impair implicit memory (Curran & Gorenstein, 1993; Sellal et al., 1992).

Could differences in peak effect have accounted for this disparity? Testing was carried out 4 hours after drug administration, as from previous studies this was deemed the most appropriate time. Data from another study using 1.5 and 3 hours testing times showed oxazepam to have a later onset of action than lorazepam (Curran et al., 1987), and lorazepam has been shown to produce more subjective sedation and psychological impairment at 4 hours than at 1.5 hours after administration (File & Bond, 1979) and so the effects of the two drugs should be equivalent at 4 hours.

The competitive task produced characteristic effects on the physiological indices. The skin conductance data showed a distinctive pattern, basal levels and reactivity increasing over the task. The drugs had no effect on the resting level, but subjects on oxazepam showed more response to events within each trial as the provocation increased, and more fluctuations at the end of the trials. Thus, the increased noise set by the subjects given lorazepam was not part of a general hyperreactivity. The heart period (inter-beat interval) changes showed distinctive patterns within trial similar to those found in our other studies. There were also changes across trial blocks. The heart period lengthened as subjects became familiar with the task and then shortened again (tachycardia) as the noise increased. Oxazepam had more effect on the resting heart period than lorazepam throughout the task but it did not block change within trial. This effect may then have been due to differences in initial values between subjects.

Pro-aggressive actions have been shown for other benzodiazepines tested in the laboratory. Chlordiazepoxide, but not oxazepam, increased hostility in a group setting after a frustrating stimulus was introduced (Gardos et al., 1968; Salzman et al., 1974; Kochansky, Salzman, Shader, Harmatz, & Ogeltree, 1975, 1977). Diazepam increased hostility in a group of females (McDonald, 1967) and behavioural aggression on the competitive reaction time task utilising shocks (Gantner & Taylor, 1988; Wilkinson, 1985). The latter study attempted to relate levels of trait anxiety to aggression, but although a relationship was found on the first block of trials (low trait anxiety subjects on diazepam showing most aggression) as provocation in the form of shock level increased, all subjects on diazepam showed greater behavioural aggression than those on placebo. The present study shows lorazepam to have similar effects to diazepam and chlordiazepoxide and confirms the finding that oxazepam does not affect behavioural aggression (Salzman et al., 1975).

The lack of anxiolytic effect of the two benzodiazepines needs comment. Such effects may not occur regularly in normal subjects with low or even moderate levels of anxiety (Spielberger et al., 1970) except under extreme anxiety-provoking conditions. But even if an anxiolytic effect is induced, aggression may increase as shown by the effects of alcohol in the study presented in Chapter 5.

SUMMARY

Two doses of two very similar benzodiazepines (oxazepam 15 and 30mg, lorazepam 1 and 2mg) and placebo were compared 4 hours post-administration on a competitive reaction time task designed to measure behavioural aggression. Forty-five subjects were assigned randomly to five independent drug groups. Subjective ratings of mood, anxiety, and aggression were completed pre- and post-drug and post-task. Oxazepam and lorazepam had very similar subjective effects but oxazepam produced more physiological reactivity. The higher dose of lorazepam increased aggressive responding on the task more than any other treatment. This may be related to the different ceiling efficacies of the two benzodiazepines.

CHAPTER SEVEN

The effects of alprazolam on behavioural aggression

INTRODUCTION

These studies were a logical extension of those presented in Chapters 5 and 6. Increased aggressive responding on laboratory tasks has been found in normal volunteers after being given chlordiazepoxide (Salzman et al., 1974), diazepam (Gantner & Taylor, 1988; Wilkinson, 1985) and lorazepam (Chapter 6). Alprazolam is a newer triazolobenzodiazepine of high potency, its anxiolytic dose being 1.5 to 3mg/day. It also has anti-panic effects at higher doses, raising the possibility of enhanced ceiling efficacy (e.g. Ballenger et al., 1988). However, it has been reported to increase verbal hostility and behavioural dyscontrol in a proportion of patients (Rosenbaum et al., 1984), especially those with borderline personality problems (Gardner & Cowdry, 1985).

One study (Pyke & Kraus, 1988) indicated that hostility was more likely to occur in patients with panic disorder or agoraphobia with panic attacks with a secondary major depressive episode. In all these trials, hostility and aggression remitted after alprazolam treatment was stopped. Thus, it was appropriate to evaluate the effects of this benzodiazepine, first in normal volunteers, and then in patients with panic disorder taking part in a therapeutic trial.

Alcohol is often associated with aggressive behaviour. In our earlier study (Chapter 5), it resulted in an anti-anxiety and anti-hostility subjective response but in increased aggressive behaviour on the competitive reaction time task. As benzodiazepines and alcohol share many pharmacological actions and anecdotally the combination is believed to result in particularly aggressive behaviour, it seemed appropriate to evaluate alprazolam alone and in combination with alcohol (but only in normal subjects) under laboratory conditions.

NORMAL SUBJECT STUDY

Methods

Subjects
Subjects were recruited via advertisements posted on the institutional notice-board. They were paid for participating. Forty-eight healthy volunteers took part in the study, 24 females and 24 males. Their mean age was 23 ± 7 and the mean weight for males was 72 ± 12kg and for females 63 ± 12kg. They were allocated randomly to one of four groups with 6 males and 6 females in each group. There were no differences between groups with respect to weight, age, or drinking behaviour.

Procedure
The study was approved by the appropriate Ethical Committee and subjects gave written, informed consent. A double-blind, independent groups design was used to compare the four treatments: alprazolam (1mg) and alcohol (0.5g/kg); alprazolam (1mg) and placebo drink; placebo capsule and alcohol (0.5g/kg); and placebo capsule and placebo drink. Alprazolam or matching placebo capsule was given by mouth after the initial testing session. Alcohol was administered 45 minutes later as vodka, made up to 250ml with low-calorie tonic. Females received a slightly lower dose of alcohol (0.42g/kg) to achieve equivalent blood alcohol concentrations to males. The placebo drink consisted of 245ml of low-calorie tonic with 5ml vodka floated on the top and wiped around the rim of the glass. Subjects were allowed 15 minutes to consume their drink. They were instructed not to drink any alcohol for 24 hours before testing and to eat only a light breakfast before reporting to the laboratory. The subjects completed the first set of measures at 9.30 a.m. Further tests were carried out at 90, 150, and 210 minutes post-drug (45, 105, and 165 minutes post-alcohol). The competitive reaction time was run at 105 minutes post-drug (60 minutes post-drink).

Measures

Breath alcohol concentration
A Lion (Cardiff, UK) Alcolmeter AE-M2 was used to estimate breath alcohol concentrations as in Chapter 5.

Competitive reaction time task (CRT)
See Chapter 3. A modification was that a total of only 19 trials was given and subjects were allowed to set the duration of noise administered. Heart period and skin conductance level were recorded throughout the task as set out in Chapter 3.

Subjective rating scales
The Mood Rating Scale, Anger Rating Scale, and Spielberger State-Trait Anxiety Inventory were completed at each time point (see Chapter 3). The Drinking Quesionnaire was filled in once, pre-drug, and the guess concerning alcohol once, 1 hour after the drink.

Analysis of data
A repeated measures multivariate analysis of variance was used: Each subject had four observations per variable for the ratings and three for the CRT. The between-subjects model was a two-by-two factorial design, the factors being alprazolam and alcohol. For the heart period, a within-subjects model of event and time was used and a priori contrasts were selected.

Results

Breath alcohol concentration
The breath alcohol concentration peaked at an equivalent mean of 71mg/100ml (blood) at 45 minutes after both alcohol alone and the combination. It declined to 42mg/100ml at 105 minutes and 28mg/100ml at 165 minutes post-alcohol, and 35mg/100ml and 24mg/100ml after the combination. There were no significant effects of alprazolam on the breath alcohol concentration.

Guess concerning alcohol
The placebo and alcohol groups differed in their detection of alcohol but the difference between the alprazolam and alcohol groups was not significant.

Competitive reaction time task

Level set – Trial 1.   There were no significant differences on Trial 1.

Trial blocks 1–3.   The levels for each group on the 19 individual trials were plotted and there was no difference in the rate of increase between groups, i.e. the lines were parallel (see Fig. 7.1). When the trials were analysed in blocks of increasing provocation, all subjects responded to provocation by increasing the level that they set through the experiment ($F_{2,43}$ = 8.77; P < 0.001), and this showed a linear trend. Subjects given the combination of alprazolam and alcohol set a higher level of noise for their opponent ($F_{1,44}$ = 9.48; P < 0.01) throughout the task (see Fig. 7.2).

Duration of noise.   Although subjects on alprazolam administered longer noises to their opponent overall, this was not significant.

Setting time.   The time the subjects took to set the noise level for their opponent decreased significantly through the experiment ($F_{2,43}$ = 4.31; P < 0.02) irrespective of drug administration.

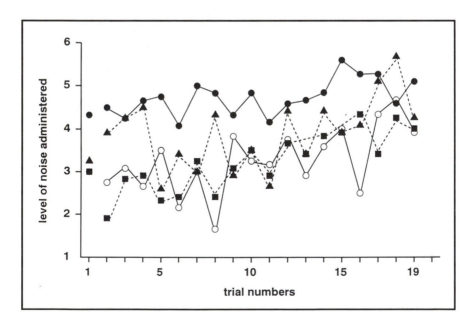

FIG. 7.1. Mean levels of noise administered by subjects to their opponent on each trial of the CRT after alprazolam (O), alcohol (■), the combination (●), and placebo (▲).

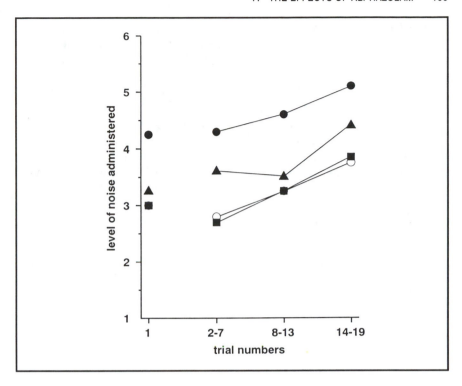

FIG. 7.2. Mean levels of noise administered by subjects to their opponent over successive blocks of trials after alprazolam (O), alcohol (■), the combination (●), and placebo (▲).

Reaction time. There was a tendency for all subjects to become faster through the task ($F_{2,43} = 3.14$; $P < 0.06$). However, subjects given alcohol were generally slower ($F_{1,44} = 8.12$; $P < 0.01$).

Physiological measures

Skin conductance level
Alprazolam decreased baseline skin conductance level ($F_{1,44} = 8.76$; $P < 0.01$). The drug also decreased the change in skin conductance level within each trial ($F_{1,44} = 9.48$; $P < 0.01$) but there were no significant changes through the experiment.

Heart period
There were no differences between groups on pre-treatment heart rate. The heart period was lengthened in all subjects 90 minutes post-administration, irrespective of group allocation.

Trial 1 (nonprovocation). The heart period shortened from immediately before the start of the trial to the later points: from the mid-trial points to after the noise and from after the warning signal for RT to after RT itself, but it lengthened from after the subjects had set the noise to be delivered to their opponent to after the display of noise they themselves were to receive. Alcohol showed a significant difference on pre-trial versus the rest of the trial. Subjects who had consumed alcohol showed less change (see Fig. 7.3). When the Trial 1 heart period was adjusted for pre-drug readings, the pre-treatment heart period was found to affect the mean level ($F_{1,43} = 8.87$; $P < 0.01$) but not the pattern of scores.

Trial blocks 1–3 (increasing provocation). Although there was a linear trend for the heart period to shorten through the experiment in

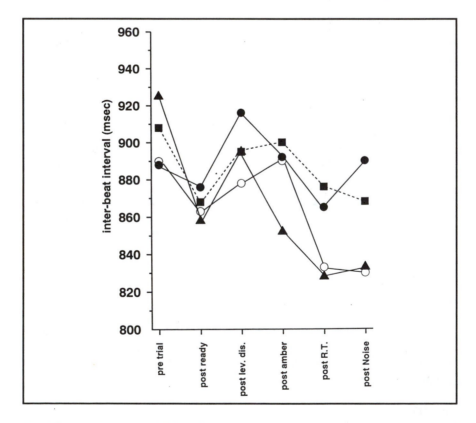

FIG. 7.3. Mean heart period (IBI) adjusted for individual pre-treatment recordings pre-trial and after events within trial for Trial 1 of the CRT after alprazolam (○), alcohol (■), the combination (●), and placebo (▲).

all groups, this was only significant for alcohol. Alcohol shortened the heart period over trial blocks ($F_{2,43}$ = 3.72; P < 0.04). There were significant differences between points measured within the trial but no change in this pattern over time. Four of the six a priori contrasts showed a significant overall effect. There was a trend for subjects who had consumed alcohol to show less change from pre-trial values to the rest of the trial ($F_{1,44}$ = 3.14; P < 0.09) but this was less pronounced than on Trial 1. When the heart period was adjusted for pre-treatment readings, it was found that although the pre-treatment reading accurately predicted later readings ($F_{1,43}$ = 15.26; P < 0.001), there was no change in the pattern.

Subjective rating scales

Drinking questionnaire
There were no differences between groups with respect to drinking behaviour.

Mood rating scale

Factor 1: alertness.   Subjects on all active treatments became drowsier (see Fig. 7.4a). This was significant after alprazolam ($F_{3,42}$ = 7.4; P < 0.001) and there was a significant drug × alcohol interaction ($F_{3,42}$ = 5.5; P < 0.01).

Factor 2: contentment.   Subjects on alcohol became significantly more contented after administration and less contented after the task ($F_{3,42}$ = 3.3; P < 0.05).

Factor 3: calmness.   All   subjects   became   less   anxious post-administration and more anxious post-task ($F_{3,42}$ = 14.0; P < 0.001) (see Fig. 7.4b).

Anger rating scale
All items on this scale showed a similar pattern. Subjects became less aggressive post-treatment and more aggressive post-task ($F_{3,42}$ = 12.01; P < 0.001) with recovery at 3.5 hours post-drug (see Fig. 7.5). There was a cubic trend.

Spielberger State-Trait Anxiety Inventory.
There was no difference between treatment groups on the STAI-Trait (mean = 39). All subjects became less anxious post-administration and more anxious post-task on the STAI-State ($F_{3,42}$ = 7.6; P < 0.001). There

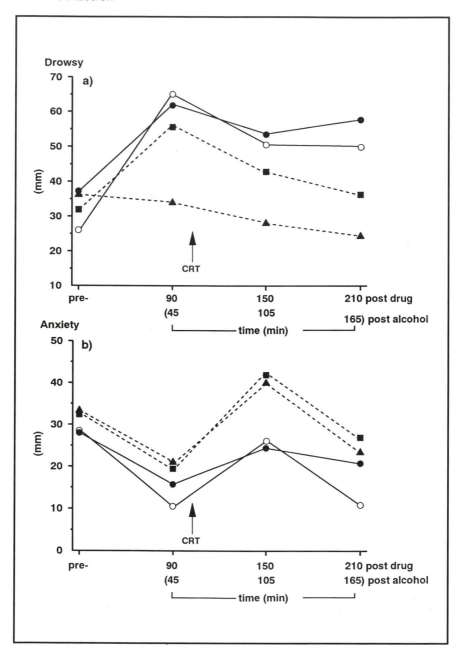

FIG. 7.4. Mean scores on (a) Factor 1 and (b) Factor 3 of the mood rating scale pre-treatment, and at 3 testing points post-treatment after alprazolam (○), alcohol (■), the combination (●), and placebo (▲).

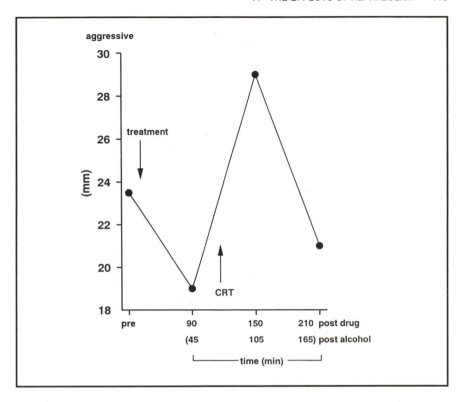

FIG. 7.5. Mean scores of all subjects are shown on the mean scale score of the anger rating scale.

was a tendency for subjects on alprazolam to show a different pattern, in that the drug blunted the anxiogenic effect of the task ($F_{3,42} = 2.59$; $P < 0.06$) but anxiety rebounded later in the day.

PATIENTS WITH PANIC DISORDER

Method

Subjects
The patients were from a treatment study of panic disorder with marked phobic avoidance described by Marks and his colleagues (1993). The 82 London patients in that study were allocated randomly to one of four treatment conditions: alprazolam and behavioural exposure, alprazolam and relaxation, placebo and exposure, placebo and relaxation.

Drugs and procedure

Only those patients who were still in the study at 8 weeks and who were prepared to come to the study site were eligible. Twenty-three patients were tested: 13 patients (5 males and 8 females with a mean age of 40.8) allocated to treatment with alprazolam and 10 patients (1 male and 9 females with a mean age of 38.5) given placebo. The data for 1 subject were lost due to equipment failure and another subject (on placebo) refused to continue after 9 trials. Complete data were therefore only available for 21 subjects (12 on alprazolam and 9 on placebo).

The study was approved by the appropriate Ethics Committee and subjects gave informed consent. Matching alprazolam (1mg) or placebo tablets were initiated under double-blind conditions at week 0 with 1 a day, rising to a maximum of 10 a day. The mean dose taken by those on alprazolam was 4.7mg/day (range 0.5–8). Patients given placebo took an average of 8.2 tablets a day (range 5–10). There were no significant differences between groups pre-treatment on a range of clinical measures, e.g. Hamilton Rating Scale of Anxiety (Hamilton, 1959), Hamilton Rating Scale of Depression (Hamilton, 1960), Beck Depression Inventory (Beck, Ward, Mendelson, Mock, & Erlbaugh, 1961), and number of major panic attacks. Subjects completed the self-ratings at entry to the study (pre-treatment) and before and after competing in the competitive reaction time task after 8 weeks of treatment.

Measures

Competitive reaction time task

See Chapter 3. Again, 19 trials were given, the task being conducted only once, after 8 weeks of treatment. No physiological measures were recorded.

Subjective rating scales

Self ratings

The mood rating scale, anger rating scale and Spielberger State-Trait Anxiety Inventory were completed (see Chapter 3).

Analysis of data

All groups were compared at baseline to assess between group differences on those ratings. Repeated measures MANOVA between subjects, drugs, psychological treatment, and time was used to analyse the ratings. However, as no effects were shown for psychological treatment, a further analysis was run on drugs and time. Contrast analysis was used to examine planned orthogonal contrasts pre-post-drug and pre-post-task. Analysis of variance between drugs was used to analyse trials 1–19 and the 3 blocks of trials of the CRT.

Results

Competitive reaction time task

Level set – Trial 1.   There were no significant differences on Trial 1.

Trial blocks 1–3.   There was a significant difference between groups over trials 2–19 ($F_{1,19}$ = 12.57; P < 0.01) (see Fig. 7.6). When the trial blocks were examined, the groups did not differ on trials 2–7 but the alprazolam group did set significantly higher volumes of noise for their opponent on trials 8–13 ($F_{1,19}$ = 14.37; P < 0.01) and trials 14–19 ($F_{1,19}$ = 12.34; P < 0.01) (see Fig. 7.7).

Setting time.   The alprazolam group tended to take longer to set the volume of noise for their opponent on the first trial ($F_{1,19}$ = 4.16; P < 0.06) but both groups accelerated through the task ($F_{1,19}$ = 9.16; P < 0.01) and there was no difference between them over trials 2–19.

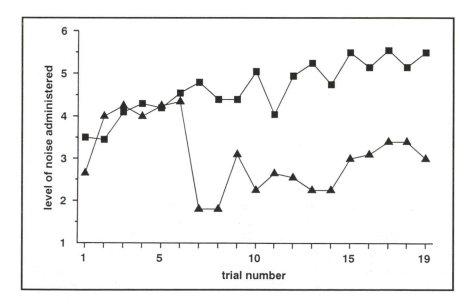

FIG. 7.6. Mean levels of noise administered by subjects to their oponent on each trial of the CRT after alprazolam (■) or placebo (▲).

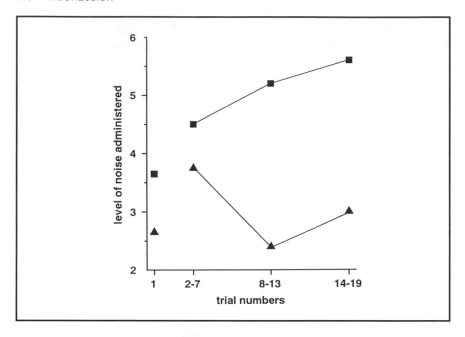

FIG. 7.7. Mean levels of noise administered by patients on alprazolam (■) or placebo (▲) to their opponent over successive blocks of trials.

Reaction time

There was no difference between groups on reaction time on Trial 1 or on the rest of the task.

Subjective rating scales

Mood rating scale

There were no significant differences between groups pre-trial.

Factor 1: alertness. There was a significant between-times effect (pre-post-task) on the lethargic–energetic scale ($F_{2,19}$ = 4.37; P < 0.03). All subjects became more energetic after the task, irrespective of drug ($F_{1,20}$ = 9.15; P < 0.01). There was a significant drug × times interaction on mentally slow–quick-witted ($F_{2,19}$ = 8.34; P < 0.01). Subjects on alprazolam rated themselves as more mentally slow after 8 weeks' treatment with the drug compared to those on placebo ($F_{1,20}$ = 13.58; P < 0.01). There were no significant effects on the overall factor score.

Factor 2: contentment. There were significant between-times effects on contented–discontented ($F_{1,20}$ = 4.16; P < 0.04) and troubled–tranquil ($F_{2,19}$ = 8.68; P < 0.01). All subjects rated themselves as more contented ($F_{1,20}$ = 5.35; P < 0.04) and more tranquil ($F_{1,20}$ = 7.82; P < 0.02) after 8 weeks' treatment with either alprazolam or placebo. The factor score showed a tendency in the same direction ($F_{2,19}$ = 2.75; P < 0.09).

Factor 3: calmness.   Comparing data at entry with that at 8 weeks, there was a significant times effect on tense–relaxed ($F_{2,19}$ = 8.6; P < 0.01). Subjects rated themselves as more relaxed after both alprazolam and placebo ($F_{1,20}$ = 15.7; P < 0.001). The factor score also showed a significant times effect ($F_{2,19}$ = 5.26; P < 0.02) in the same direction.

Anger rating scale
Two scales showed a significant difference between groups before trial. The group who were allocated to alprazolam rated themselves as more sociable ($F_{1,20}$ = 5.7; P < 0.03) and more friendly ($F_{1,20}$ = 6.18; P < 0.03) than the placebo group. An analysis of covariance, adjusting for pre-values, was therefore run on these two scales. There were no times effects or interactions but there was an overall drug effect on friendly–hostile ($F_{1,19}$ = 17.25; P < 0.001), which was significant on the covariance analysis. There was no such effect on sociable–unsociable. Two other scales showed an overall drug effect. Subjects rated themselves as more tolerant ($F_{1,20}$ = 5.01; P < 0.04) and pleased ($F_{1,20}$ = 9.23; P < 0.01) on alprazolam compared to placebo. Subjects on alprazolam also tended to rate themselves as less aggressive on the mean of all 13 scales but this failed to reach significance ($F_{1,20}$ = 3.77; P < 0.07). There were no differences between groups after the task.

Spielberger State-Trait Anxiety Inventory
Subjects only completed these scales at week 8, so there were no pre-treatment scores. There were no significant differences between groups after 8 weeks' treatment. The alprazolam group scored 52.5 ± 11.3 on the STAI-Trait and 43.6 ± 10.8 on the STAI-State, and the corresponding scores for the placebo group were 47.1 ± 11.7 and 46.9 ± 12.2.

DISCUSSION

None of the normal subjects were abstainers and all claimed to drink within the recommended limits. Alprazolam did not affect the breath alcohol concentrations but it did raise the amount of self-rated intoxication. It also increased ratings of sedation but these were not potentiated by the combined treatment. Anxiety was blunted by the alprazolam but hostility after the task was unaffected. Anxiety increased again 3.5 hours after the drug as its effects wore off but this may have been a harbinger of rebound. Discontent was noted only in subjects who had consumed alcohol, perhaps as the intoxication wore off.

The general pattern of effects was consistent throughout the competitive task as the level of provocation increased. All subjects decreased the time taken to choose a level of noise for their opponent and decreased the time taken to respond in an attempt to win the competition, although subjects who had consumed alcohol were generally slower. All subjects also set increased levels of noise for their opponent as the level that they themselves received increased, and the rate of increase in the four groups was similar. Subjects given either alcohol or alprazolam alone set no higher levels of noise for their opponent than subjects on placebo. Indeed, the levels set by these three groups on individual trials often overlapped, but the levels set by the group who had received both alprazolam and alcohol were higher than all other groups on 17 of the 19 trials.

The physiological effects during the task followed a similar pattern as in our other studies but the effects of the treatments differed. Increasing provocation tended to increase cardiac activity but only after alcohol. This drug is known to quicken the heart. In our study, alcohol reduced the change from pre- to within-trial periods. Subjects after alcohol therefore showed a stress-response dampening (SRD) effect, both with and without alprazolam. The effects of benzodiazepines on heart-rate are generally inconsistent (Hoehn-Saric & McLeod, 1986) but they have been shown to lower skin conductance (Albus et al., 1986). Alprazolam decreased both the SC resting level and the within-trial change and thus exerted a SRD action. However, neither alprazolam nor alcohol alone increased the level of noise set by the subjects for their opponent. Only the combination had this effect. The combination group who showed most behavioural aggression also revealed an SRD effect on both cardiac and electrodermal activity and showed decreased anxiety. It may be that a treatment that decreases physiological and subjective responses to stress facilitates an aggressive response to provocation. It has been suggested that alcohol-induced anxiety reduction is accompanied by a decrease in aggressive restraints (Horton, 1943).

A moderate dose of alcohol was used to represent what a person being prescribed a benzodiazepine might cautiously consume at a social event, but in fact subjects consuming alcohol alone did not respond more aggressively than those on placebo. Comparing the results with our previous experiments, the alcohol group actually responded more aggressively than a group previously administered 0.25g/kg of alcohol (Chapter 5) but the placebo group was more aggressive. In previous experiments, the placebo groups have been more comparable, averaging a noise level of less than 3 over 3 trial blocks, but in this experiment they started off at over 3 and increased to over 4. It is not known why the current placebo group should be more aggressive, but nevertheless the combination increased aggression more than would have been predicted by the summation of the two individual treatments. This result confirms that the behavioural aggression reported after the combination of alcohol and alprazolam (Terrell, 1988) can be modelled in healthy volunteers in the laboratory.

The second alprazolam study accords with previous clinical reports of increased hostility and aggression after taking this drug. Although patients given alprazolam were more aggressive behaviourally throughout the task, this was not significant on the pre-provocation trial, i.e. before they knew what level of noise their opponent would set for them, or when they received only low volumes of noise if they lost the competition. In fact, the two groups increased in parallel at this point. However, when the noise intensified, the patients taking alprazolam continued to increase the level they set, whereas those on placebo decreased the level. The patients taking alprazolam were thus much more likely to respond to provocation. This was similar to the pattern of effects after a single 2mg dose of lorazepam (Chapter 6). Unfortunately a gender bias occurred in the random allocation of subjects to alprazolam or placebo in this study. There was only one male in the placebo group but five in the alprazolam group. In previous studies on benzodiazepines and aggression no sex differences have been found (see Chapter 6; Taylor & Chermack, 1993). However, we decided to examine the data more closely for two reasons. First, healthy male subjects behave more aggressively in response to provocation than female subjects after alcohol (Chapter 5) and second, as more women present with anxiety disorders, they are also more likely to be prescribed drugs like alprazolam. We analysed the data for the 16 females separately, but the results closely resembled the original analysis. Again, no difference was found on the first seven trials but the patients on alprazolam set significantly higher levels of noise for their opponent on both later blocks ($P < 0.05$). This is based on a rather small number of subjects but shows that the full result was not an artefact due to gender.

Interestingly, the behavioural aggression shown in this study was not accompanied by subjective ratings of increased anger or hostility. In contrast, the group taking alprazolam tended to note less aggression, rating themselves as more tolerant, friendly, and pleased. This kind of dissociation between behaviour and feelings has been noted before after consuming alcohol (Chapter 5) and is likely to reflect a lack of insight. Most case reports detailing extreme aggressive behaviour after the consumption of benzodiazepines describe accompanying anger. However, studies that report specifically on extreme rage or physical assaults tend to underestimate the number of patients who may display a general increase in aggressiveness or irritability without recognising any emotional changes or link to medication (Dietch & Jennings, 1988). Such patients may maintain that the drug calms them down. The present study used a parallel groups design. Recently case reports have accrued of anger attacks as a component of untreated panic disorder (Fava et al., 1990) and of major depressive disorder (Fava et al., 1993). Therefore, the patients allocated to alprazolam might be more likely to display aggression, irrespective of drug treatment. This seems unlikely as the patients were matched pre-treatment on a number of clinical indices. Dosage is a crucial element in our findings. The mean dose of 4.7mg was the same as that used by Gardner and Cowdry (1985). Early reports of rage attacks were often related to high doses, and problems with triazolam have been blamed on exceeding the clinically recommended dose (*Drug and Therapeutics Bulletin*, 1991). Plasma concentrations of alprazolam have been found to relate not only to treatment response but also to the emergence of adverse reactions (Lesser et al., 1992) and it is possible that increased hostility and aggression occur above a certain threshold. However, Lesser et al. (1992) found considerable between-patient variability, indicating that some individuals may be more likely to display such behaviour at doses within the recommended therapeutic range. Increasing the dose may therefore just augment the number of people susceptible to such effects.

SUMMARY

Forty-eight moderate social drinkers were assigned to one of four treatments: alprazolam (1mg) and alcohol (0.5g/kg); alprazolam (1mg) and placebo drink; placebo capsule and alcohol (0.5g/kg); and placebo capsule and placebo drink. Breath alcohol concentrations and ratings of mood and intoxication were completed at 90, 150 and 210 minutes post-drug (45, 105, and 165 minutes post-alcohol). Subjects competed in a competitive reaction time task at 105 minutes post-drug (60 minutes post-alcohol) during which psychophysiological measures were simultaneously monitored. Active treatments increased sedation and intoxication and the task increased feelings of hostility and anxiety in all subjects. Aggressive responding increased in all groups in response to provocation, but some stress response dampening was shown after both alcohol and alprazolam on the psychophysiological measures and after alprazolam on subjective ratings of anxiety. The combination of alprazolam and alcohol increased behavioral aggression more than would have been predicted from the sum of the single effects, confirming clinical reports of behavioural dyscontrol.

Twenty-three patients with a diagnosis of panic disorder with agoraphobia were randomly assigned to 8 weeks' treatment with alprazolam or placebo. They filled in self-ratings before and after treatment and competed on a competitive reaction time task, designed to measure behavioural aggression, after 8 weeks' treatment. Patients taking both alprazolam and placebo rated decreased anxiety after 8 weeks' treatment but those on alprazolam also tended to report less hostility. On the behavioural task patients on alprazolam behaved more aggressively in response to provocation. This is the first study to confirm clinical reports of benzodiazepine-induced dyscontrol on an objective laboratory measure.

CHAPTER EIGHT

General discussion and conclusions

The incidence of both physical and verbal aggression is of wide concern. In the minds of the mass media and the general public it is often associated with mental illness. However, although violence can be associated with florid symptoms of a psychiatric disorder, this is in fact rare. More commonly, severe aggression is associated with a diagnosis of personality disorder and with alcohol or substance abuse. The personality disorders most commonly associated with hostility and aggression are antisocial or borderline. These diagnoses imply a malfunctioning of learned social behaviour as well as experiencing extreme anger or responding aggressively to minimal provocation. Such behaviours or feelings are perhaps better understood in dimensional rather than categorical terms. Thus, the dimension of hostility may range from someone who is difficult to please to someone who can be extremely violent. There is evidence that traits of aggressiveness and hostility are partially inherited and correlational studies have linked traits to biological indices. The clearest relationship to be isolated so far has been that of diminished 5-HT metabolism in the central nervous system (CNS) with the dysregulation of aggression. A hostility syndrome with many biobehavioural components has been proposed (Williams, 1994). In this model, a deficient CNS 5-HT system is seen to underlie increased anger and irritability, increased sympathetic nervous system (SNS) reactivity, decreased parasympathetic nervous system activation, and increased alcohol consumption, as well as increased eating and smoking behaviour. Alcohol has a long history of association with aggression but other substance abuse has also been implicated. There is some evidence that alcohol and/or substance abuse and adult aggression have common antecedents. Thus, as well as personality traits, factors such as perinatal difficulties, family conflict, childhood neglect or abuse, and school failure are very important in the history of habitually aggressive people.

THE MEASUREMENT OF AGGRESSION

Aggressive behaviour is both multicausal and multifaceted, but in order to study it, we have to break it down into components and find ways in which to measure these. It is important to examine both what people say they do and how they behave in a particular situation. The majority of work on aggression has concentrated on questionnaire data, but laboratory tasks allow the precise measurement of aggressive responding while eliminating the possibility of actual harm. The current work then describes a specific experimental technique to measure behavioural aggression in the laboratory. We modified an already existing laboratory task both to make it ethically more acceptable and to make it more like everyday experience. Noise is now a common noxious stimulus, especially when viewed as a threat, but shock is rarely encountered.

The first question we posed was would behavioural responding on this task relate to aggressive behaviour outside the laboratory, i.e. did it demonstrate external validity? Our major finding was that it did. Forensic patients with a history of aggression responded more aggressively on the task than either healthy controls or psychiatric patients without a specific history of aggression. Thus, people who display aggressive behaviour in ordinary life also show it in the laboratory.

We examined factors that might have contributed to this behaviour, such as mood and physiological state of activation. Berkowitz (1993) has proposed that negative affect is an important influence on aggressive behaviour. However, the behaviour of the forensic patients could not be explained by negative mood alone as although the psychiatric patients showed more dysphoria, anxiety, and irritability than the healthy subjects, the forensic patients did not differ from the control patients on these measures. Nor could the behaviour be explained by physiological differences in levels of activation. Some work has suggested that habitual criminals show a history of underarousal on both central and peripheral measures from adolescence (Raine et al., 1990). However, this work examined the incidence of all serious offending. In this context aggressive behaviour is likely to have been primarily instrumental rather than affective (see p.2). Concentrating on affective aggression, Zillman (1988) has claimed that high sympathetic excitation may impair cognitive appraisal and guidance of behaviour leading to a greater likelihood of aggression. Both our patient groups exhibited higher levels of physiological activation before and during the task but there were only minor differences between groups. In fact, the forensic patients were more similar to healthy controls in their reactivity to trial events on the CRT. Thus, their levels of SNS excitation were no higher than the other groups. However, this does not preclude them from being somehow more sensitive to similar levels of dysphoric mood and both central and peripheral arousal. In contrast to patients with panic disorder, who are hypothesised to interpret such symptoms as indicating impending danger to their own physical or mental health, aggressive patients may be keen to seek an external or interpersonal cause for their negative feelings and physiological activation so that they can attribute blame, and attack.

The second question posed was would a questionnaire measure of aggression differentiate between the groups? The BDHI was selected as the best validated measure (Edmunds & Kendrick, 1980) and it was found to discriminate between them; the forensic patients admitted to exhibiting more "motor aggression" and feeling more suspicious than both other groups, confirming earlier findings with other aggressive populations (Lothstein & Jones, 1978; Renson et al., 1978). The motor aggression factor of the BDHI also correlated with trait measures of anxiety and anger. Therefore, the aggressive patients generally felt both more threatened by others and more hostile towards them. This kind of aggressive disposition is compatible with the expression of a hostile attributional bias postulated to develop early in life (Dodge, 1993; Nasby et al., 1979). Aggressive response patterns are learned and encoded in memory in childhood. These "scenarios" are rehearsed (Huesmann & Eron, 1984) and therefore readily retrievable in situations in which provocation or attack are perceived. The CRT created these conditions in the laboratory, and in combination with dysphoric mood and high levels of peripheral and central activation, led to increased aggression by the forensic group. This is in line with Berkowitz's (1993) theory that people with a hostile disposition and who have learned patterns of aggressive behaviour are more likely to be aggressive under conditions leading to increased arousal and anger.

We attempted to control the current social status of the subjects so that the groups did not differ on demographic features. The differences in aggression are therefore likely to be more deep-seated, due to hereditary or early developmental influences. The fewer years of education in the forensic group may have been due either to pre-existing interpersonal difficulties or to poor cognitive development, but in any case add to the complex interaction between hereditary and environmental factors leading to habitual aggressive behaviour.

THE PSYCHOLOGICAL EFFECTS OF ALCOHOL

As mentioned before, alcohol has long been recognised as a contributory factor in aggressive behaviour. Our groups did not differ on current alcohol intake and few had a history of alcohol or substance abuse and so these factors could not have accounted for their behaviour on the task. Nevertheless, alcohol may have played a part in past aggressive acts. Having shown that the CRT was sensitive to individual differences in aggressive disposition, we wanted to see if it would prove sensitive to the effects of alcohol in healthy volunteer subjects. Although the consumption of alcohol has been persistently linked to aggressive behaviour, such behaviour is not an automatic consequence of drinking and the actual factors involved in alcohol-induced aggression are difficult to pinpoint. One of the important psychological factors appears to be the perception of threat or provocation. Thus, an early study that examined the effects of alcohol on performance on the Buss aggression machine (see p.53) found that it did not increase aggressive responding (Bennett, Buss, & Carpenter, 1969). In contrast, studies using the CRT with increasing levels of provocation (shock delivery) have shown alcohol to consistently increase aggressive responding (Shuntich & Taylor, 1972; Taylor & Gammon, 1975; Taylor, Schmutte, Leonard, & Cranston, 1979). These results were found to be related to dose as only the high dose increased aggression, and only male subjects were used. In the first experiment reported here (Chapter 5), we confirmed that a moderate dose of alcohol did indeed increase aggressive responding compared to placebo. As in previous experiments (Taylor & Chermack, 1993), we found that intoxicated subjects initiated aggressive behaviour. Both male and female subjects on the higher dose of alcohol set moderate levels of noise for their opponents on the first trial, pre-provocation, and both continued to set these levels for the first block of trials despite receiving much lower levels themselves. Males and females then showed a different pattern. Females kept to moderate settings, whereas males continued to escalate the levels they administered. Previous studies have not examined concurrent mood. We found that not only did alcohol exert some calming, anxiolytic effect before the task when the subjects rated themselves as more calm, tranquil, and friendly than those on placebo, but the increase in aggression was not accompanied by corresponding increases in hostile or dysphoric mood and alcohol showed a stress response dampening effect on cardiac activity. It is important to note that these subjects were normal, healthy social drinkers with no history of aggressive behaviour, yet they behaved very aggressively on this laboratory task.

There are many theories relating to alcohol's effects on aggression (Gustafson, 1993). These results do not support the disinhibition model as the subjects' behaviour was not totally disinhibited. They in fact increased their aggression as the provocation increased. Neither do the results accord with the arousal model. Although physiological arousal was generally increased by alcohol, responses to particular points of stress within the experiment were in fact decreased. The expectancy model does not appear to account completely for our results. Most of our subjects believed that they had consumed some alcohol but not all groups behaved aggressively. Also, if subjects expect to behave aggressively after consuming alcohol, then they might also be expected to rate themselves as more aggressive. Our results offer most support to cognitive theories that suggest that alcohol is consumed to reduce self-awareness (Hull, 1981) or that it reduces attentional capacity, so that attention is directed to the most salient external cues and away from subtle inhibitory cues (Taylor & Leonard, 1983). A similar explanation has been termed "alcoholic myopia" by Steele and Josephs (1990) who suggest that alcohol both restricts attention to immediate situational cues and reduces the ability to process this information fully.

Despite a lack of direct evidence on some aspects, a number of researchers now feel that their results fit most clearly into this kind of explanation (e.g. Gustafson, 1993). Alcohol is postulated to impair higher-order information processing (Peterson, Rothfleisch, & Zelazco, 1990), which may in turn reduce inhibitory control and attention to inhibitory cues. Alcohol has in fact been shown to make subjects report being more externally orientated on a state locus of control scale (Gustafson, 1993). In our experiment, by reducing both negative mood and physiological reaction to negative events, alcohol rendered the subjects less aware of themselves and less responsive to situational norms of appropriate behaviour. They then concentrated on task variables such as increasing provocation. It has been postulated that this effect may be greater for groups who are habitually more likely to express aggression during the provocation stage (Taylor & Chermack, 1993). In groups in whom sanctions against aggressive behaviour are stronger, it may be more difficult to overcome inhibitory cues and this may account for the lesser effect in women (Gomberg, 1993).

THE PHARMACOLOGICAL EFFECTS OF ALCOHOL

The theories mentioned so far concentrate on the psychological effects of alcohol but attempts are now being made to link these in with its pharmacological actions (Pihl, Peterson, & Lau, 1993). Alcohol has effects on subtypes of 5-HT, NMDA, and GABA receptors (Miczek et al., 1993). It is not known what the respective roles of these actions are in heightening aggression and it is likely to be due to a complex interaction. However, the anxiolytic effect of alcohol is probably due to its action on GABA. By enhancing the inhibitory action of GABA, alcohol reduces the inhibitory effect that fear exercises on behaviour in response to threat or possible punishment (Gray, 1987). This in turn may encourage the expression of aggressive behaviour that is normally inhibited and this effect is likely to be strongest in individuals with readily available aggressive response patterns.

THE EFFECTS OF ANXIOLYTICS AND ALCOHOL

Benzodiazepines bind to receptor sites on the inhibitory GABA$_A$-chloride complex. They maximise the normally occurring GABA-mediated inhibition and therefore exert powerful anxiolytic effects. However, whereas work with alcohol has shown consistent aggression-enhancing effects under conditions of provocation (Bushman & Cooper, 1990), work with benzodiazepines has revealed differences among them. Oxazepam, in particular, has not been shown to increase aggression (Salzman et al., 1975). We therefore set out to investigate if we could replicate these effects on the CRT. We compared two very similar compounds and confirmed that oxazepam did not increase aggression, neither dose differing from placebo. At the low dose, the chemically very similar lorazepam also showed no effects but the high dose increased aggression more than any other condition. Neither benzodiazepine exerted a stress-response dampening effect and they did not differ in their effects on mood; so increased aggression was not related to any anxiolytic effect nor to increased anger or excitation. This disproportionate effect of lorazepam is not confined to aggressive behaviour. It has been shown not only to have more general effect on memory function (Curran et al., 1987) but also to impair different functions, e.g. priming (Curran & Gorenstein, 1993; Sellal et al., 1992), and to cause more withdrawal problems (Tyrer et al., 1981). Although lorazepam has a very similar structure to oxazepam, it is 15 times more potent. Other high-potency compounds have also exhibited more problems, with adverse effects such as amnesia, disinhibition, and aggression, especially at high doses (*Drug and Therapeutics Bulletin*, 1991; Martinez-Cano et al., 1995). We therefore went on to examine the effects of another high-potency benzodiazepine.

Alprazolam is a newer triazolobenzodiazepine compound of high potency. It is not only used to treat generalised anxiety but in high doses also to combat panic and this has led to reports of increased hostility and aggression (Gardner & Cowdry, 1985; Pyke & Kraus, 1988; Rosenbaum et al., 1984). We found a low dose of alprazolam to have only minimal effects on aggression and hostility, but when combined with a low dose of alcohol, the picture changed dramatically. The combination increased aggressive responding more than any of the other treatments. This effect was not accompanied by any increase in reported anger or hostility, and anxiety was decreased compared to the other conditions. The combination also exerted a stress-response dampening effect on both cardiac and electrodermal activity. These effects were then similar but more powerful than the previous findings with a moderate dose of alcohol. The combination of alcohol and a high-potency benzodiazepine may therefore reduce both self-awareness and attention to inhibitory cues to a greater extent, thus facilitating the expression of aggressive behaviour. It has been shown that the aggression of intoxicated subjects can be controlled by redirecting their attention away from instigative cues towards normative, socially appropriate standards of behaviour (Jeavons & Taylor, 1985) but it is not known if this would be possible with benzodiazepine-facilitated aggression.

It has been suggested that benzodiazepines only increase aggression in people with a predisposition to hostility. However, both verbal and behavioural aggression have been reported in a proportion of patients with anxiety disorders with no previous history of such behaviour (Rosenbaum et al., 1984). Our study with patients with panic disorder confirmed these findings. These patients had no history of aggressive behaviour or increased hostility yet the patients on alprazolam showed significantly more behavioural aggression on the CRT than those taking placebo. As previously, subjects on the benzodiazepine did not exhibit more behavioural aggression pre-provocation or when they received the minimal levels of provocation. They responded aggressively to provocation but as with lorazepam, this behaviour was not accompanied by any reported increase in anger or hostility. This kind of dissociation then confirms a lack of insight or reduced self-awareness. In fact, three factors seem to be important in recognising benzodiazepine-linked aggression. First, it occurs in response to provocation; second, it is recognised by others and not complained of by the patients themselves; and third it is more likely to occur with higher doses. An additional fourth factor may be important but needs further investigation: Reports of increased hostility and aggression tend to occur more often after taking high potency compounds like alprazolam, triazolam, lorazepam, and clonazepam.

Anxiety disorders are reported to be more prevalent among females (Reich, 1986) and so benzodiazepines are more commonly prescribed for women. Most of the patients in the alprazolam study were female but this did not affect the results. In fact, we found no sex differences in any of the studies with benzodiazepines in contrast to alcohol. The lesser effect of alcohol on aggression in women has been explained by sex differences in the expression of aggression (Eron, 1987). When presented with situations designed to elicit anger (e.g. strong criticism), women are more likely to express feelings of hurt or disappointment (Brody, 1985). It may be that by decreasing these alternative feelings, benzodiazepines allow anger to be expressed, or it may be that taking a pill to lessen anxiety and reduce self-awareness legitimises aggressive behaviour.

Differences have been shown between the effects of alcohol and benzodiazepines on the CRT. Benzodiazepines did not increase aggression pre-provocation in contrast to alcohol. Healthy control subjects who are untreated or on placebo are not impaired cognitively and are thus aware of implicit norms of acceptable behaviour. They both assume that the opponent will not try to harm them on the initial trial and realise the potential consequences of provoking the opponent. They therefore set low levels of noise. During the provocation stage, as the intensity of noise given escalates, the (nonintoxicated) subjects become sensitive to instigative cues and attribute hostile intent to their opponent. They then increase their settings gradually but rarely exceed the level administered to them, in order to avoid provoking the opponent further. Subjects with a hostile disposition, like the forensic patients described here, are not excessively aggressive when no threat cues are present (pre-provocation) but respond to the perceived hostile intent of their opponent and attempt to affect their behaviour by attacking more. Subjects on benzodiazepines presumably feel quite calm and unthreatened initially and so set low intensities of noise. However, when they perceive hostile intent they ignore situational norms of appropriate behaviour and also attack. In contrast to these groups, intoxicated subjects initiate aggressive behaviour on the first trial. This behaviour is not totally disinhibitory, only moderate levels are set, but they do not reduce in response to very low levels administered to them but selectively attend to any provocation and attack. There is some evidence that healthy subjects with a hostile disposition, as measured on the BDHI, attack more under provocation when they have consumed alcohol (Bailey & Taylor, 1991). Alcohol then seems to exert most effect in people who have patterns of aggressive behaviour readily available and under conditions that minimise awareness of inhibitory social cues. The combination of alcohol and a benzodiazepine, however, results in both initiation of attack and continued escalation of aggressive behaviour. The influence of hostile disposition is less apparent, perhaps because expectancy is less important, and so sex differences are eradicated.

ANIMAL MODELS

Recent work in animals has attempted to examine the pharmacology behind alcohol's effects on aggression. Research has followed two separate strands, investigating GABA and 5-HT. It has been found that mice with high or low levels of aggressive behaviour as a result of selected breeding can be further differentiated by benzodiazepine receptor binding at the $GABA_A$ receptor complex (Miczek et al., 1993). Confirming our findings in humans, aggression induced by low doses of alcohol has been found to be potentiated by BZD agonists in mice, but in addition, BZD antagonists have been shown to be capable of reversing it. It may be, therefore, that BZD antagonists, like flumazenil, would also be able to reverse aggression induced by BZD agonists. However, there is some controversy over whether they are able to reverse fully the cognitive effects of some compounds (Kapczinski, Curran, Gray, & Lader, 1994) and the picture may be similar with aggressive behaviour.

The aggression-enhancing effects of benzodiazepines and alcohol may not be primarily mediated by GABA. Benzodiazepines have also been shown to reduce 5-HT function by enhancing dendritic release of 5-HT (Soubrié, Blas, Ferron, & Glowinski, 1983) and to decrease 5-HT turnover and release (Pratt, Jenner, & Marsden, 1985). Abnormalities of the serotonin system have been shown to relate to hostility and aggression. Most of the human work linking deficient levels of central 5-HT with aggressive behaviour has been correlational, relating biochemical indices to aggressive traits or past behaviour (see p.34) and there has been very little work examining current behaviour. Depletion of the 5-HT precursor, tryptophan, allows us to examine, by implication, the effects of depleted central 5-HT on current feelings and behaviour, but it may be necessary to both manipulate trait characteristics and provoke aggressive behaviour. Confirming this, a recent study has found a tryptophan deficient amino acid drink to increase both feelings of hostility and aggressive responding on the CRT in subjects with high scores on the BDHI (Cleare & Bond, 1995).

Animal studies have set out to examine the effects of manipulating 5-HT on alcohol-induced aggression. It has been found that tryptophan can partially block alcohol-induced aggression in mice (Wagner, Fisher, Pole, Borve, & Johnson, 1993). Serotonergic drugs such as fluoxetine and fenfluramine were also found to reduce substantially aggressive behaviour in the same series of studies. Little work has so far examined the role of 5-HT in alcohol-induced aggression in humans. However, a recent study investigated the effects of a moderate dose (0.8g/kg) of alcohol on both tryptophan concentrations and the ratio of tryptophan to the sum of the five amino acids that compete with tryptophan for the same cerebral uptake mechanism (Badawy, Morgan, Lovett, Bradley, & Thomas, 1995). Both total serum tryptophan and the ratio were significantly decreased by alcohol. Circulating tryptophan available to the brain was therefore reduced, resulting in reduced central 5-HT synthesis. The authors present their results as a possible biological explanation of the incidence of aggressive behaviour following the consumption of alcohol.

CONCLUSION

In summary, cognitive theories of aggressive behaviour emphasise the emotional and cognitive processes underlying such behaviour. In order to study these processes in more detail, we need to develop new methods of measuring interpersonal aggression in the field and in the laboratory. Aggression is primarily a social behaviour and the way in which people appraise a situation will influence how they feel and behave. Drugs that impair an individual's ability to process socially relevant information may lower the threshold at which aggressive behaviour is likely to occur. Serotonin is involved in the regulation of complex, intelligent, adaptive behaviour and is thought to be an important mediator of control over premature responding. Deficiencies in the central serotonergic system, whatever their origin, may lead to both increased hostility and an increased likelihood of responding aggressively to minimal provocation, i.e. before appropriate evaluation of all the information available. Newer, more specific serotonergic drugs may be able to reverse this by decreasing hostility and facilitating delay, thus allowing full appraisal of the situation. However, other neurotransmitter systems may also be involved. It is only by continuing to study the complex interaction between pharmacological and psychological factors that we will gain more insight into the mechanisms underlying aggressive behaviour.

References

Abelson, R.P. (1981). Psychological status of the script concept. *American Psychologist, 36,* 715–729.

Addad, M., Benezech, M., Bourgeois, M., & Yesavage, J. (1981). Criminal acts among schizophrenics in French mental hospitals. *Journal of Nervous and Mental Disease, 169,* 289–293.

Adler, H., & Lidberg, L. (1995). Characteristics of repeat killers in Sweden. *Criminal Behaviour and Mental Health, 5,* 9–13.

Albus, M., Stahl, S., Müller-Spahn, F., & Engel, R.R. (1986). Psychophysiological differentiation of two types of anxiety and its pharmacological modification by minor tranquillizer and beta-receptor-blocker. *Biological Psychology, 23,* 39–51.

Alpert, M., Allan, E.R., Citrome, L., Laury, G., Sison, C., & Sudilovsky, A. (1990). A double-blind, placebo-controlled study of adjunctive nadolol in the management of violent psychiatric patients. *Psychopharmacology Bulletin, 26,* 367–371.

American Psychiatric Associaton. (1994). *Diagnostic criteria from DSM-IV.* Washington, DC: American Psychiatric Association.

Apter, A., van Praag, H.M., Plutchik, R., Sevy, S., Korn, M., & Brown, S.-L. (1990). Interrelationships among anxiety, aggression, impulsivity, and mood: a serotonergically linked cluster? *Psychiatry Research, 32,* 191–199.

Arora, C., & Meltzer, H.Y. (1989). Serotonergic measures in the brains of suicide victims: $5-HT_2$ binding sites in the frontal cortex of suicide victims and control subjects. *American Journal of Psychiatry, 146,* 730–736.

Asberg, M., Schalling, D., Traskman-Bendz, L., & Wagner, A. (1987). Psychobiology of suicide, impulsivity, and related phenomena. In H.Y. Meltzer (Ed.), *Psychopharmacology: The third generation of progress.* New York: Raven Press.

Asberg, M., Thoren, P., & Traskman, L. (1976a). "Serotonin depression"—biochemical subgroup with the affective disorders? *Science, 191,* 478–480.

Asberg, M., Traskman, L., & Thoren, P. (1976b). 5–HIAA in the cerebrospinal fluid: a suicide predictor? *Archives of General Psychiatry, 33,* 1193–1197.

Averill, J.R. (1974). An analysis of psychophysiological symbolism and its influence on emotions. *Journal for the Theory of Social Behaviour, 4,* 147–190.

Ax, A.F. (1953). The psychophysiological differentiation between fear and anger in humans. *Psychosomatic Medicine, 15,* 433–442.

Bach-Y-Rita, G. (1974). Habitual violence and self-mutilation. *American Journal of Psychiatry, 131,* 1018–1020.

Bach-Y-Rita, G., & Veno, A. (1974). Habitual violence: a profile of 62 men. *American Journal of Psychiatry, 131,* 1015–1017.

Badawy, A.A.-B., Morgan, C.J., Lovett, J.W.T., Bradley, D.M., & Thomas, R. (1995). Decrease in circulating tryptophan availability to the brain after acute ethanol consumption by normal volunteers: implications for alcohol-induced aggressive behaviour and depression. *Pharmacopsychiatry, 28 (Suppl.),* 93–97.

Bailey, D.S., & Taylor, S.P. (1991). Effects of alcohol and aggressive disposition on human physical aggression. *Journal of Research on Personality, 25,* 334–342.

Bailey, D.S., Leonard, K.E., Cranston, J.W., & Taylor, S.P. (1983). Effects of alcohol and self-awareness on human physical aggression. *Personality and Social Psychology Bulletin, 9,* 289–295.

Bales, R.F. (1950). *Interaction process analysis.* Reading, MA: Addison-Wesley.

Ballenger, J.C., Burrows, G.D., Dupont, R.L., et al. (1988). Alprazolam in panic disorder and agoraphobia: results from a multicenter trial: I. Efficacy in short-term treatment. *Archives of General Psychiatry, 45,* 413–422.

Balon, R. (1990). Buspirone for attention deficit hyperactivity disorders. *Journal of Clinical Psychopharmacology, 10,* 77.

Bancroft, J., & Backstrom, T. (1985). Premenstrual syndrome. *Clinical Endocrinology, 22,* 313–336.

Bandura, A. (1973). *Aggression: A social learning analysis.* Englewood Cliffs, NJ: Prentice-Hall.

Bandura, A. (1977). *Social learning theory.* Englewood Cliffs, NJ: Prentice-Hall.

Bandura, A., Ross, D., & Ross, S.A. (1963). Imitation of film-mediated aggressive models. *Journal of Abnormal and Social Psychology, 66,* 3–11.

Banki, C.M., Arato, M., Papp, Z., & Kurcz, M. (1984). Biochemical markers in suicidal patients. Investigations with cerebrospinal fluid amine metabolites and endocrine tests. *Journal of Affective Disorders, 6,* 341–350.

Barker, R., Dembo, T., & Lewin, K. (1941). Frustration and regression: An experiment with young children. *University of Iowa Studies in Child Welfare, no. 18.*

Baron, R.A. (1972). Aggression as a function of ambient temperature and prior anger arousal. *Journal of Personality and Social Psychology, 21,* 183–189.

Baron, R.A. (1977). *Human aggression.* New York and London: Plenum.

Baron, R.A. (1978). Aggression-inhibiting influence of sexual humour. *Journal of Personality and Social Psychology, 36,* 189–197.

Baron, R.A. (1989). Personality and organizational conflict: Effects of the Type A behavior pattern and self-monitoring. *Organizational Behavior and Human Decision Processes, 44,* 281–297.

Baron, R.A., & Ball, R.L. (1974). The aggression-inhibiting influence of nonhostile humor. *Journal of Experimental Social Psychology, 10,* 23–33.

Baron, R.A., & Bell, P.A. (1975). Aggression and heat: Mediating effects of prior provocation and exposure to an aggressive model. *Journal of Personality and Social Psychology, 31,* 825–832.

Baron, R.A., & Bell, P.A. (1976). Aggression and heat: The influence of ambient temperature, negative affect, and a cooling drink on physical aggression. *Journal of Personality and Social Psychology, 33,* 245–255.

Baron, R.A., & Richardson, D.R. (Eds.) (1994). *Human aggression* (2nd ed.). New York: Plenum.

Bear, D.M., & Fedio, P. (1977). Quantitative analysis of interictal behavior in temporal lobe epilepsy. *Archives of Neurology, 33,* 454–467.

Beck, A.T. (1967). *Depression: Clinical, experimental and theoretical aspects.* New York: Hoeber.

Beck, A.T., Ward, C.H., Mendelson, M., Mock, J.E., & Erlbaugh, J.K. (1961). An inventory for measuring depression. *Archives of General Psychiatry, 4,* 561–571.

Benezech, M., Bourgeois, M., & Yesavage, J. (1980). Violence in the mentally ill: a study of 547 patients at a French hospital for the criminally insane. *Journal of Nervous and Mental Disease, 168,* 698–700.

Bennett, R.M., Buss, A.H., & Carpenter, J.A. (1969). Alcohol and human physical aggression. *Quarterly Journal of Studies on Alcohol, 30,* 870–877.

Berkowitz, L. (1962). *Aggression: A social psychological analysis.* New York: McGraw-Hill.

Berkowitz, L. (1964). Aggressive cues in aggressive behavior and hostility catharsis. *Psychological Review, 71,* 104–122.

Berkowitz, L. (1969). The frustration-aggression hypothesis revisited. In L. Berkowitz (Ed.), *Roots of aggression.* New York: Atherton.

Berkowitz, L. (1974). Some determinants of impulsive aggression: The role of mediated associations with reinforcements for aggression. *Psychological Review, 81,* 165–176.

Berkowitz, L. (1983). Aversively stimulated aggression: some parallels and differences in research with animals and humans. *American Psychologist, 38,* 1135–1144.

Berkowitz, L. (1984). Some effects of thoughts on anti- and prosocial influences of media events: A cognitive-neoassociationist analysis. *Psychological Bulletin, 95,* 410–427.

Berkowitz, L. (1989). The frustration-aggression hypothesis: examination and reformulation. *Psychological Bulletin, 106,* 59–73.

Berkowitz, L. (1993). *Aggression. Its causes, consequences, and control.* New York: McGraw-Hill.

Berkowitz, L., & Geen, R.G. (1967). Stimulus qualities of the target of aggression: A further study. *Journal of Personality and Social Psychology, 5,* 364–368.

Berkowitz, L., & LePage, A. (1967). Weapons as aggression-eliciting stimuli. *Journal of Personality and Social Psychology, 7,* 202–207.

Berkowitz, L., Corwin, R., & Heironimus, M. (1962). Film violence and subsequent aggressive tendencies. *Public Opinion Quarterly, 27,* 217–229.

Bernstein, I.S., Richardson, D., & Hammock, G. (1987). Convergent and discriminant validity of the Taylor and Buss measures of physical aggression. *Aggressive Behavior, 13,* 15–24.

Blackburn, R. (1971). Personality types among abnormal homicides. *British Journal of Criminology, 11,* 14–31.

Blackburn, R. (1982). *The special hospitals assessment of personality and socialisation.* Unpublished manuscript, Park Lane Hospital, Liverpool.

Blackburn, R. (1986). Patterns of personality deviation among violent offenders: replication and extension of an empirical taxonomy. *British Journal of Criminology, 26,* 254–269.

Blackburn, R. (1993). Psychopathic disorder, personality disorders and aggression. In C. Thompson & P. Cowen (Eds.), *Violence. Basic and clinical science.* Oxford: Butterworth Heinemann.

Blackburn, R., & Lee-Evans, J.M. (1985). Reactions of primary and secondary psychopaths to anger-evoking situations. *British Journal of Clinical Psychology, 24,* 93–100.

Blackshear, M.A., Steranka, L.R., & Sanders-Bush, E. (1981). Multiple serotonin receptors: regional distribution and effect of raphe lesions. *European Journal of Pharmacology, 76,* 325–334.

Bohman, M., Cloninger, C., Sigvardsson, S., & von Knorring, A.L. (1982). Predisposition to petty criminality in Swedish adoptees: Genetic and environmental heterogeneity. *Archives of General Psychiatry, 39,* 1133–1141.

Bond, A.J., & Lader, M.H. (1974). The use of analogue scales in rating subjective feelings. *British Journal of Medical Psychology, 47,* 211–218.

Bond, A.J., & Lader, M.H. (1979). Benzodiazepines and aggression. In M. Sandler (Ed.), *Psychopharmacology of aggression.* New York: Raven Press.

Bond, A.J., & Lader, M.H. (1986). A method to elicit aggressive feelings and behaviour via provocation. *Biological Psychology, 22,* 69–79.

Bond, A.J., James, D.C., & Lader, M.H. (1974). Physiological and psychological measures in anxious patients. *Psychological Medicine, 4,* 364–373.

Bond, A., Shine, P., & Bruce, M. (1995). Validation of visual analogue scales in anxiety. *International Journal of Methods in Psychiatric Research, 5,* 1–9.

Borden, R.J. (1975). Witnessed aggression: Influence of an observer's sex and values on aggressive responding. *Journal of Personality and Social Psychology, 31,* 567–573.

Botha, M.P., & Mels, G. (1990). Stability of aggression among adolescents over time: A South African study. *Aggressive Behavior, 16,* 361–380.

Boyatzis, R.E. (1983). Who should drink what, when, and where if looking for a fight. In E. Gottheil, K.A. Druley, T.E. Skoloda & H.M. Waxman (Eds.), *Alcohol, drug abuse and aggression.* Springfield, IL: Charles C. Thomas.

Boyle, D., & Tobin, J.M. (1961). Pharmaceutical management of behaviour disorders: chlordiazepoxide in covert and overt expressions of aggression. *Journal of the Medical Society of New Jersey, 58,* 427–4

Brock, T.C., & Buss, A.H. (1964). Effects of justification for aggression and communication with the victim on post aggression dissonance. *Journal of Abnormal and Social Psychology, 68,* 403–412.

Brody, L.R. (1985). Gender differences in emotional development: A review of theories and research. *Journal of Personality, 53,* 102–149.

Brown, G.L., Ebert, M.H., Goyer, P.F., et al. (1982). Aggression, suicide and serotonin: relationship to CSF amine metabolites. *American Journal of Psychiatry, 139,* 741–746.

Brown, G.L., & Goodwin, F.K. (1984). Diagnostic, clinical and personality characteristics of aggressive men with low CSF 5-HIAA. *Clinical Neuropharmacology, 7,* 756–757.

Brown, G.L., Goodwin, F.K., Ballenger, J.C., Goyer, P.F., & Major, L.F. (1979). Aggression in humans correlates with cerebrospinal fluid amine metabolites. *Psychiatry Research, 1,* 131–139.

Brown, G.L., & Linnoila, M.I. (1990). CSF serotonin metabolite (5–HIAA) studies in depression, impulsivity and violence. *Journal of Clinical Psychiatry, 51 (Suppl. 4),* 31–41.

Bruce, M., & Lader, M. (1991). DSM-III-R state anxiety symptoms in anxiety disorder patients. *Biological Psychiatry, 30,* 519–522.

Bryant, J., & Zillmann, D. (1979). Effect of intensification of annoyance through unrelated residual excitation on substantially delayed hostile behaviour. *Journal of Experimental Social Psychology, 15,* 470–480.

Burnstein, E., & Worchel, P. (1962). Arbitrariness of frustration and its consequences for aggression in a social situation. *Journal of Personality, 30,* 528–540.

Bushman, B.J., & Cooper, H.M. (1990). Effects of alcohol on human aggression: an integrative research review. *Psychological Bulletin, 107,* 1–15.

Bushman, B.J., & Geen, R.G. (1990). Role of cognitive-emotional mediators and individual differences in the effects of media violence on aggression. *Journal of Personality and Social Psychology, 58,* 156–163.

Buss, A.H. (1961). *The psychology of aggression.* New York: Wiley.

Buss, A.H. (1963). Physical aggression in relation to different frustrations. *Journal of Abnormal and Social Psychology, 67,* 1–7.

Buss, A.H. (1966). The effect of harm on subsequent aggression. *Journal of Experimental Research in Personality, 1,* 249–255.

Buss, A.H., & Durkee, A. (1957). An inventory for assessing different kinds of hostility. *Journal of Consulting Psychology, 11,* 343–349.

Buss, A.H., & Perry, M. (1992). Personality processes and individual differences; the aggression questionnaire. *Journal of Personality and Social Psychology, 63,* 452–459.

Caine, T.M., Foulds, G.A., & Hope, K. (1967). *Manual of the hostility and direction of hostility questionnaire (H.D.H.Q.).* London: University of London Press.

Campbell, A., Bibel, D., & Muncer, S. (1985). Predicting our own aggression: Person, subculture, or situation? *British Journal of Social Psychology, 24,* 169–180.

Cantor, J.R., Zillman, D., & Einsiedel, E.F. (1978). Female responses to provocation after exposure to aggressive and erotic films. *Communication Research, 5,* 395–411.

Caprara, G.V., Cinanni, V., D'Imperio, G., Passerini, S., Renzi, P., & Travaglia, G. (1985). Indicators of impulsive aggression: Present status of research on irritability and emotional susceptibility scales. *Personality and Individual Differences, 6,* 665–674.

Caprara, G.V., Renzi, P., Alcini, P., D'Imperio, G., & Travaglia, G. (1983). Instigation to aggress and escalation of aggression examined from a personological perspective: The role of irritability and of emotional susceptibility. *Aggressive Behavior, 9,* 345–351.

Carver, C.S., & Glass, D.C. (1978). Coronary-prone behavior pattern and interpersonal aggression. *Journal of Personality and Social Psychology, 36,* 361–366.

Cherek, D.R. (1981). Effects of smoking different doses of nicotine on human aggressive behavior. *Psychopharmacology, 75,* 339–349.

Cherek, D.R., Steinberg, J.L., & Manno, B.R. (1985). Effects of alcohol on human aggressive behaviour. *Journal of Studies on Alcohol, 46,* 321–328.

Christmas, A.J., & Maxwell, D.R. (1970). A comparison of the effects of some benzodiazepines and other drugs on aggressive and exploratory behaviour in mice and rats. *Neuropharmacology, 9,* 17–29.

Clarke, D.D., & Hoyle, R. (1988). A theoretical solution to the problem of personality-situational interaction. *Personality and Individual Differences, 9,* 133–138.

Clarke, A.S., Kammerer, C.M., George, K.P., et al. (1995). Evidence for heritability of biogenic amine levels in the cerebrospinal fluid of rhesus monkeys. *Biological Psychiatry, 38,* 572–577.

Cleare, A.J., & Bond, A.J. (1995). The effect of tryptophan depletion and enhancement on subjective and behavioural aggression in normal male subjects. *Psychopharmacology, 118,* 72–81.

Cleare, A.J., & Bond, A.J. (1997). Does central serotonergic function correlate inversely with aggression? A study using d-felfluramine in healthy subjects. *Psychiatry Research.*

Cloninger, C.R., Bohman, M., & Sigvardsson, S. (1981). Inheritance of alcohol abuse: cross fostering analysis of alcoholic men. *Archives of General Psychiatry, 38,* 861–868.

Coccaro, E.F., & Astill, J.L. (1990). Central serotonin function in parasuicide. *Progress in Neuropsychopharmacology and Biological Psychiatry, 14,* 663–674.

Coccaro, E.F., & Bergeman, C.S. (1993). Heritability of irritable impulsiveness: a study of twins reared together and apart. *Psychiatry Research, 48,* 229–242.

Coccaro, E.F., Kavoussi, R.J., & Lesser, J.C. (1992). Self and other directed human aggression: The role of the central serotonergic system. *International Clinical Psychopharmacology, 6 (Suppl. 6),* 70–83.

Coccaro, E.F., Kramer, E., Zemishlany, Z., et al. (1990). Pharmacologic treatment of noncognitive behavioral disturbances in elderly demented patients. *American Journal of Psychiatry, 147,* 1640–1645.

Coccaro, E.F., Lawrence, T., Trestman, R., Gabriel, S., Klar, H.M., & Siever, L.J. (1991). Growth hormone responses to intravenous clonidine challenge correlates with behavioral irritability in psychiatric patients and in healthy volunteers. *Psychiatry Research, 39,* 129–139.

Coccaro, E.F., & Siever, L.J. (1995). The neuropsychopharmacology of personality disorders. In F.E. Bloom & D.J. Kupfer (Eds.), Psycopharmacology: The fourt generation of progress. New York: Raven Press.

Coccaro, E.F., Siever, L.J., Klar, H.M., Maurer, G., Cochrane, K., Cooper, T.B. Mohs R.C., & Davis, K.L. (1989). Serotonergic studies in patients with affective and personality disorders. *Archives of General Psychiatry, 46,* 587–599.

Coccaro, E.F., Silverman, J.M., Klar, H.M., Horvath, T.B., & Siever, L.J. (1994). Familial correlates of reduced central serotonergic system function in patients with personality disorders. *Archives of General Psychiatry, 51,* 318–324.

Cohen, M.J., Schandler, S.L., & Naliboff, B.D. (1983). Psychophysiological measures from intoxicated and detoxified alcoholics. *Journal of Studies on Alcohol, 44,* 271–282.

Colenda, C.C. (1988). Buspirone in treatment of agitated demented patient. *Lancet, I,* 1169.

Collins, J.J., Jr. (Ed.) (1981). *Drinking and crime: Perspectives on the relationship between alcohol consumption and criminal behavior.* New York: Guilford Press.

Collins, J.J., & Schlenger, W.E. (1988). Acute and chronic effects of alcohol use on violence. *Journal of Studies on Alcohol, 49,* 516–521.

Conger, J.J. (1956). Alcoholism: theory, problem, and challenge. II. Reinforcement theory and the dynamics of alcoholism. *Quarterly Journal of Studies on Alcohol, 17,* 296–305.

Conn, P.J., & Sanders-Bush, E. (1986). Regulation of serotonin-stimulated phosphoinositide hydrolysis: relationship to the 5–HT$_2$ binding site. *Journal of Neuroscience, 6,* 3669–3675.

Conners, C.K., Kramer, R., Rothschild, G.H., Schwartz, L., & Stone, A. (1971). Treatment of young delinquent boys with diphenylhydantoin sodium and methylphenidate. *Archives of General Psychiatry, 24,* 156–160.

Cornelius, J.R., Soloff, P.H., Perel, J.M., et al. (1991). A preliminary trial of fluoxetine in refractory borderline patients. *Journal of Clinical Psychopharmacology, 11,* 116–120.

Court-Brown, W.M. (1968). Males with an XYY sex chromosome complement. *Journal of Medical Genetics, 5,* 341–359.

Cowdry, R.W., & Gardner, D.L. (1988). Pharmacotherapy of borderline personality disorder: alprazolam, carbamazepine, trifluoperazine and tranylcypromine. *Archives of General Psychiatry, 45,* 111–119.

Craig, T.J. (1982). An epidemiological study of problems associated with violence among psychiatric inpatients. *American Journal of Psychiatry, 139,* 1262–1266.

Crow, T.J., Cross, A.J., Cooper, S.J., et al. (1984). Neurotransmitter receptors and monoamine metabolites in brains of patients with Alzheimer-type dementia and depression, and suicides. *Neuropharmacology, 23,* 1561–1569.

Curran, H.V., & Gorenstein, C. (1993). Differential effects of lorazepam and oxazepam on priming. *International Clinical Psychopharmacology, 8,* 37–42.

Curran, H.V., Schiwy, W., & Lader, M. (1987). Differential amnesic properties of benzodiazepines: a dose-response comparison of two drugs with similar elimination half-lives. *Psychopharmacology, 92,* 358–364.

Dabbs, J.M., Jr., Frady, R.L., Carr, T.S., & Besch, N.F. (1987). Saliva testosterone and criminal violence in young adult prison inmates. *Psychosomatic Medicine, 49,* 174–182.

Dalton, K. (1977). *The premenstrual syndrome and progesterone therapy.* London: Heinemann.

Daly, R.F. (1969). Neurological abnormalities in XYY males. *Nature, 221,* 472–473.

Dantzer, R. (1977). Behavioral effects of benzodiazepines: a review. *Biobehavioural Reviews, 1,* 71–86.

Darby, B.W., & Schlenker, B.R. (1982). Children's reactions to apologies. *Journal of Personality and Social Psychology, 43,* 742–753.

Delgado-Escueta, A., Mattson, R., & King, L. (1981). The nature of aggression during epileptic seizures. *New England Journal of Medicine, 305,* 711–716.

Deluty, R.H. (1985). Consistency of assertive, aggressive, and submissive behavior for children. *Journal of Personality and Social Psychology, 49,* 1054–1065.

Dengerink, H.A. (1971). Anxiety, aggression and physiological arousal. *Journal of Experimental Research in Personality, 5,* 223–232.

Dengerink, H.A., & Fagan, N.J. (1978). Effect of alcohol on emotional responses to stress. *Journal of Studies on Alcohol, 39,* 525–539.

Depue, R.A., & Spoont, M.R. (1986). Conceptualizing a serotonin trait: a behavioural dimension of constraint. *Annals of New York Academy of Sciences, 487,* 47–62.

Devinsky, O., & Bear, D. (1984). Varieties of aggressive behavior in temporal lobe epilepsy. *American Journal of Psychiatry, 141,* 651–656.

Diamond, E.L., Schneiderman, N., Schwartz, D., Smith, J.C., Vorp, R., & Pasin, R.D. (1984). Harassment, hostility, and Type A as determinants of cardiovascular reactivity during competition. *Journal of Behavioral Medicine, 7,* 171–189.

Dietch, J.T., & Jennings, R.K. (1988). Aggressive dyscontrol in patients treated with benzodiazepines. *Journal of Clinical Psychiatry, 49,* 184–188.

DiMascio, A., Shader, R.I., & Harmatz, J. (1969). Psychotropic drugs and induced hostility. *Psychosomatics, 10,* 46–47.

Dodge, K.A. (1980). Social cognition and children's aggressive behavior. *Child Development, 51,* 162–170.

Dodge, K.A. (1993). Studying mechanisms in the cycle of violence. In C. Thompson & P. Cowen (Eds.), *Violence. Basic and clinical science.* Oxford: Butterworth Heinemann.

Dodge, K.A., & Coie, J.D. (1987). Social information-processing factors in reactive and proactive aggression in children's peer groups. *Journal of Personality and Social Psychology, 53,* 1146–1158.

Dodge, K.A., Murphy, R.R., & Buchsbaum, K. (1984). The assessment of intention-cue detection skills in children: Implications for developmental psychopathology. *Child Development, 55,* 163–173.

Dodge, K.A., Price, J.M., Bachorowski, J.-A., & Newman, J.P. (1990a). Hostile attributional biases in severely aggressive adolescents. *Journal of Abnormal Psychology, 99,* 385–392.

Dodge, K.A., Bates, J.E., & Pettit, G.S. (1990b). Mechanisms in the cycle of violence. *Science, 250,* 1678–1683.

Dollard, J., Doob, L.W., Miller, N.E., Mowrer, O.H., & Sears, R.R. (1939). *Frustration and aggression.* New Haven, CT: Yale University Press.

Drug and Therapeutics Bulletin (1991). The sudden withdrawal of triazolam— reasons and consequences. *Drug and Therapeutics Bulletin, 29,* 89–90.

Duncan, B.L. (1976). Differential social perception and attribution of intergroup violence: Testing the lower limits of stereotyping of blacks. *Journal of Personality and Social Psychology, 34,* 590–598.

Duncan, P., & Hobson, G.N. (1977). Toward a definition of aggression. *Psychological Records, 3,* 545–553.

Eagly, A.H., & Steffen, F.J. (1986). Gender and aggressive behavior: A meta-analytic review of the social psychological literature. *Psychological Bulletin, 100,* 309–330.

Edmunds, G., & Kendrick, D. (1980). *The measurement of human aggressiveness.* Chichester, UK: Horwood.

Ehrenkranz, J., Bliss, E., & Sheard, M.H. (1974). Plasma testosterone: Correlation with aggressive behavior and social dominance in man. *Psychosomatic Medicine, 36,* 469–475.

Eichelman, B. (1987). Neurochemical and psychopharmacologic aspects of aggressive behaviour. In H. Y. Meltzer (Ed.), *Psychopharmacology: The third generation of progress.* New York: Raven Press.

Eichelman, B. (1988). Toward a rational pharmacotherapy for aggressive and violent behaviour. *Hospital and Community Psychiatry, 39,* 31–39.

Eichelman, B., & Hegstrand, L. (1982). Stress-induced alterations in aggression and brain biochemistry. Presented at the 13th Collegium Internationale Neuro-Psychopharmacologicum, Jerusalem, Israel.

Ellinwood, E.H. (1971). Assault and homicide associated with amphetamine abuse. *American Journal of Psychiatry, 127,* 90–95.

Elliott, F.A. (1977). Propranolol for the control of belligerent behavior following acute brain damage. *Annals of Neurology, 1,* 489–491.

Epstein, S., & Taylor, S.P. (1967). Instigation to aggression as a function of degree of defeat and perceived aggressive intent of the opponent. *Journal of Personality, 35,* 265–289.

Erdmann, G., & van Lindern, B. (1980). The effects of beta-adrenergic stimulation and beta-adrenergic blockade on emotional reactions. *Psychophysiology, 17,* 332–338.

Eron, L.D. (1987). The development of aggressive behavior from the perspective of a developing behaviorism. *American Psychologist, 42,* 435–442.

European Rating Aggression Group (ERAG) (1992). Social dysfunction and aggression scale (SDAS-21) in generalized aggression and in aggressive attacks: A validity and reliability study. *International Journal of Methods in Psychiatric Research, 2,* 15–29.

Eves, F.F., & Gruzelier, J.H. (1984). Individual differences in the cardiac response to high intensity auditory stimulation. *Psychophysiology, 21,* 342–352.

Fagan, J. (1990). Intoxication and aggression. In M.H. Tonry & J.Q. Wilson (Eds.), *Drugs and crime. Crime and justice, vol. 13.* Chicago: University of Chicago Press.

Faretra, G. (1981). A profile of aggression from adolescence to adulthood. *American Journal of Orthopsychiatry, 51,* 439–453.

Farmer, R. (1987). Hostility and deliberate self-poisoning. The role of depression. *British Journal of Psychiatry, 150,* 609–614.

Fava, M., Anderson, K., & Rosenbaum, J.F. (1990). "Anger attacks": possible variants of panic and major depressive disorders. *American Journal of Psychiatry, 147,* 867–870.

Fava, M., Rosenbaum, J.F., Pava, J.A., McCarthy, M.K., Steingard, R.J., & Bouffides, E. (1993). Anger attacks in unipolar depression, part 1: Clinical correlates and response to fluoxetine treatment. *American Journal of Psychiatry, 150,* 1158–1163.

Fehr, R.S., & Stern, J.A. (1970). Peripheral psychological variables and emotion: the James-Lange theory revisited. *Psychological Bulletin, 74,* 411–424.

Felson, R.B. (1982). Impression management and the escalation of aggression and violence. *Social Psychology Quarterly, 45,* 245–254.

Felson, R.B. (1984). Patterns of aggressive social interaction. In A. Mummendey (Ed.), *Social psychology of aggression: From individual behavior to social interaction.* Berlin: Springer-Verlag.

Fenwick, P. (1986). Aggression and epilepsy. In H. Bolwig & M. Trimble (Eds.), *Aspects of epilepsy and psychiatry.* Chichester: Wiley.

Ferguson, T.J., & Rule, B.G. (1980). Effects of inferential set, outcome severity, and basis for responsibility on children's evaluations of aggressive acts. *Developmental Psychology, 16,* 141–146.

Ferguson, S.M., Rayport, M., & Corrie, W.S. (1986). Brain correlates of aggressive behaviour in temporal lobe epilepsy. In B.K. Doanne & K.E. Livingston (Eds.), *The limbic system: functional organisation and clinical disorders.* New York: Raven Press.

Ferguson, T.J., Rule, B.G., & Lindsay, R.C. (1982). The effects of caffeine and provocation of aggression. *Journal of Research in Personality, 16,* 60–71.

Feshbach, S. (1964). The function of aggression and the regulation of aggressive drive. *Psychological Review, 71,* 257–272.

Feshbach, S. (1970). Aggression. In P.H. Mussen (Ed.), *Carmichael's manual of child psychology.* New York: Wiley.

Feshbach, S., & Price, J. (1984). Cognitive competencies and aggressive behavior: A developmental study. *Aggressive Behavior, 10,* 185–200.

Festinger, L. (1957). *A theory of cognitive dissonance.* Stanford, CA: Stanford University Press.

File, S.E., & Bond, A.J. (1979). Impaired performance and sedation after a single dose of lorazepam. *Psychopharmacology, 66,* 309–313.

Fottrell, E. (1980). A study of violent behavior among patients in psychiatry hospitals. *British Journal of Psychiatry, 136,* 216–221.

Foulds, G.A. (1965). *Personality and personal illness.* London: Tavistock Press.

Fowles, D.C. (1980). The three arousal model: implications of Grays' two-factor learning theory for heart rate, electrodermal activity, and psychopathy. *Psychophysiology, 17,* 87–104.

Fowles, D.C. (1986). The eccrine system and electrodermal activity. In M.G.H. Coles, E. Donchin, & S.W. Porges (Eds.), *Psychophysiology: Systems, processes, and applications.* New York: Guilford Press.

Freud, S. (1920). *A general introduction to psycho-analysis.* New York: Boni & Liveright.

Fritze, J., Sofic, E., Muller, T., Pfuller, H., Lanczik, M., & Riederer, P. (1990). Cholinergic-adrenergic balance, part 2: relationship between drug sensitivity and personality. *Psychiatry Research, 34,* 271–279.

Frodi, A., Macaulay, J., & Thome, P.R. (1977). Are women always less aggressive than men? A review of the experimental literature. *Psychological Bulletin, 84,* 634–660.

Fromm, E. (1973). *The anatomy of human destructiveness.* New York: Holt, Rinehart & Winston.

Frost, W.D., & Averill, J.R. (1982). Differences between men and women in the everyday experience of anger. In J.R. Averill (Ed.), *Anger and aggression. An essay on emotion.* New York: Springer-Verlag.

Funkenstein, D.H., King, S.H., & Drolette, M.E. (1954). The direction of anger during a laboratory stress-inducing situation. *Psychosomatic Medicine, 16,* 404–413.

Gaebelein, J.W., & Hay, W.W. (1975). The effects of verbal and behavioral non-compliance on third party instigation of aggression. *Journal of Research in Personality, 9,* 113–121.

Gale, A., & Edwards, J.A. (1983). Introduction. In A. Gale & J.A. Edwards (Eds.), *Physiological correlates of human behaviour, Vol.II.* London: Academic Press.

Gantner, A.B., & Taylor, S.P. (1988). Human physical aggression as a function of diazepam. *Personality and Social Psychology Bulletin, 14,* 479–484.

Gantner, A.B., & Taylor, S.P. (1992). Human physical aggression as a function of alcohol and threat of harm. *Aggressive Behaviour, 18,* 29–36.

Gardner, D.L., & Cowdry, R.W. (1985). Alprazolam-induced dyscontrol in borderline personality disorder. *American Journal of Psychiatry, 142,* 98–100.

Gardos, G., DiMascio, A., Salzman, C., & Shader, R.I. (1968). Differential actions of chlordiazepoxide and oxazepam in hostility. *Archives of General Psychiatry, 18,* 758–760.

Geen, R.G. (1968). Effects of frustration, attack and prior training in aggressiveness upon aggressive behavior. *Journal of Personality and Social Psychology, 9,* 316–321.

Geen, R.G. (1976). *Personality, the skein of behaviour.* St. Louis, MO: Mosby Company.

Geen, R.G. (1978). Effects of attack and uncontrollable noise on aggression. *Journal of Research in Personality, 12,* 15–29.

Geen, R.G., & Berkowitz, L. (1967). Some conditions facilitating the occurrence of aggression after the observation of violence. *Journal of Personality, 35,* 666–676.

Geen, R.G., & O'Neal, E.C. (1969). Activation of cue-elicited aggression by general arousal. *Journal of Personality and Social Psychology, 11,* 289–292.

Geen, R.G., Rakosky, J.J., & Pigg, R. (1972). Awareness of arousal and its relation to aggression. *British Journal of Social and Clinical Psychology, 11,* 115–121.

Genthner, R.W., & Taylor, S.P. (1973). Physical aggression as a function of racial prejudice and the race of the target. *Journal of Personality and Social Psychology, 27,* 207–210.

Gentry, W.D. (1970). Effects of frustration, attack and prior aggressive training on overt aggression and vascular processes. *Journal of Personality and Social Psychology, 16,* 718–725.

Geyer, M.A., & Segal, D.S. (1974). Shock-induced aggression: opposite effects of intra-ventricularly infused dopamine and norepinephrine. *Behavioral Biology, 10,* 99–104.

Gilman, A.G., Mayer, S.E., & Melmon, K.L. (1980). Pharmacodynamics. In L.S. Goodman & A. Gilman (Eds.), *The pharmacological basis of therapeutics* (6th ed.). New York: Macmillan.

Glennon, R.A. (1990). Serotonin receptors: clinical implications. *Neuroscience and Biobehavioural Reviews, 14,* 35–47.

Glitz, D.A., & Pohl, R. (1991). $5-HT_{1A}$ partial agonists. What is their future? *Drugs, 41,* 11–18.

Goldberg, S.C., Shulz, S.C., Shulz, P.N., Resnick, R.J., Haymer, R.M., & Friedelro, R.O. (1986). Borderline and schizotypal personality disorders treated with low dose of thiothixene versus placebo. *Archives of General Psychiatry, 43,* 580–586.

Gomberg, E.S.L. (1993). Alcohol, women and the expression of aggression. *Journal of Studies on Alcohol, Suppl. 11,* 85–95.

Graham, M.A. (1988). Misuse of midazolam. *Journal of Clinical Psychiatry, 49,* 244.

Graham, F.K., & Clifton, R.K. (1966). Heart-rate change as a component of the orienting response. *Psychological Bulletin, 65,* 305–320.

Gray, J.A. (1975). *Elements of a two-process theory of learning.* New York: Academic Press.

Gray, J.A. (1987). *The psychology of fear and stress* (2nd ed.). New York: Cambridge University Press.

Greenblatt, D.J., Shader, R.I., Divoll, M., & Harmatz, J.S. (1981). Benzodiazepines: a summary of pharmacokinetic properties. *British Journal of Clinical Pharmacology, 11,* 11S–16S.

Greendyke, R.M., & Kanter, D.R. (1986). Therapeutic effects of pindolol on behavioral disturbances associated with organic brain disease: a double-blind study. *Journal of Clinical Psychiatry, 47,* 423–426.

Greendyke, R.M., Kanter, D.R., Schuster, D.B., Verstreate, S., & Wooton, J. (1986). Propranolol treatment of assaultive patients with organic brain disease. A double-blind crossover, placebo-controlled study. *Journal of Nervous and Mental Disease, 174,* 290–294.

Greendyke, R.M., Schuster, D.B., & Wooton, J.A. (1984). Propranolol in the treatment of patients with organic brain disease. *Journal of Clinical Psychopharmacology, 4,* 282–285.

Greenwell, J., & Dengerink, H.A. (1973). The role of perceived versus actual attack in human physical aggression. *Journal of Personality and Social Psychology, 26,* 66–71.

Gross-Isseroff, R., Israeli, M., & Biegon, A. (1989). Autoradiographic analysis of tritiated imipramine binding in the human brain post mortem: effects of suicide. *Archives of General Psychiatry, 46,* 237–241.

Grossman, S.P. (1963). Chemically induced epileptiform seizures in the cat. *Science, 142,* 409–411.

Gualtieri, C.T., & Schroeder, S.R. (1989). Pharmacotherapy for self-injurious behavior: preliminary tests of the D1 hypothesis. *Psychopharmacology Bulletin, 25,* 364–371.

Gudelsky, G.A., Koenig, J.I., & Meltzer, H.Y. (1986). Thermoregulatory responses to serotonin (5–HT) receptor stimulation in the rat: evidence for opposing roles of $5-HT_2$ and $5-HT_{1A}$ receptors. *Neuropharmacology, 25,* 1307–1313.

Gunn, J., & Robertson, G. (1976). Psychopathic personality: a conceptual problem. *Psychological Medicine, 6,* 631–634.

Gustafson, R. (1985). Alcohol-related aggression: a further study of the importance of frustration. *Psychological Reports, 57,* 683–697.

Gustafson, R. (1986). Alcohol, aggression and the validity of experimental paradigms with women. *Psychological Reports, 59,* 51–56.

Gustafson, R. (1992). Alcohol and aggression: A replication study controlling for potential confounding variables. *Aggressive Behavior, 18,* 21–28.

Gustafson, R. (1993). What do experimental paradigms tell us about alcohol-related aggressive responding? *Journal of Studies on Alcohol, Suppl. 11,* 20–29.

Hamilton, M. (1959). The assessment of anxiety states by rating. *British Journal of Medical Psychology, 32,* 50–55.

Hamilton, M. (1960). A rating scale for depression. *Journal of Neurology, Neurosurgery and Psychiatry, 23,* 56–62.

Hanssen, T., Heyden, T., Sundberg, I., Alfredsson, G., Nybäck, H., & Wetterberg, L. (1980). Propranolol in schizophrenia: clinical, metabolic and pharmacological findings. *Archives of General Psychiatry, 37,* 685–690.

Harre, R., & Lamb, R. (1983). *The encyclopedia dictionnaire of psychology.* Oxford: Blackwell.

Harrington, M.A., Zhong, P., Garlow, S.J., & Ciaranello, R.D. (1992). Molecular biology of serotonin receptors. *Journal of Clinical Psychiatry, 53 (Suppl. 10),* 8–27.

Harris, M.B. (1973). Field studies of modeled aggression. *Journal of Social Psychology, 89,* 131–139.

Harris, M.B. (1974). Mediators between frustration and aggression in a field experiment. *Journal of Experimental Social Psychology, 10,* 561–571.

Harris, M.B., & Huang, L.C. (1974). Aggression and the attribution process. *Journal of Social Psychology, 92,* 209–216.

Healy, D. (1990). The psychopharmacological era: notes towards a history. *Journal of Psychopharmacology, 4,* 152–167.

Herbert, J. (1993). The neuroendocrinology of aggression: Roles of steroids, monoamines and peptides. In C. Thompson & P. Cowen (Eds.), *Violence: basic and clinical science.* Oxford: Butterworth Heinemann.

Hermann, B.P., & Whitman, S. (1984). Behavioral and personality correlates of epilepsy: a review, methodological critique and conceptual model. *Psychological Bulletin, 95,* 451–497.

Hoehn-Saric, R., & McLeod, D.R. (1986). Physiological and performance responses to diazepam: Two types of effects. *Psychopharmacology Bulletin, 22,* 439–443.

Honigfeld, G., Gillies, R.D., & Klett, C.J. (1976). NOSIE. Nurses' Observation Scale for Inpatient Evaluation. In W. Guy (Ed.), *ECDEU assessment manual for psychopharmacology.* Rockville, MD: NIAAA.

Horton, D. (1943). The functions of alcohol in primitive societies: A cross-cultural study. *Quarterly Journal of Studies in Alcohol, 4,* 199–220.

Hoyer, D., Pazos, A., Probst, A., & Palacios, J.M. (1986). Serotonin receptors in human brain. I. Characterization and autoradiographic localisation of 5HT-1A recognition sites. Apparent absence of 5HT-1B sites. *Brain Research, 376,* 85–96.

Huesmann, L.R., & Eron, L.D. (1984). Cognitive processes and the persistence of aggressive behavior. *Aggressive Behavior, 10,* 243–251.

Huesmann, L.R., & Eron, L.D. (Eds.) (1986). *Television and the aggressive child: A cross-national comparison.* Hillsdale, NJ: Lawrence Erlbaum Associates Inc.

Hull, J.G. (1981). A self-awareness model of the causes and effects of alcohol consumption. *Journal of Abnormal Psychology, 90,* 586–600.

Hyde, J.S. (1984). How large are gender differences in aggression? A developmental meta-analysis. *Developmental Psychology, 20,* 722–736.

Hynan, D.J., & Grush, J.E. (1986). Effects of impulsivity, depression, provocation, and time on aggressive behavior. *Journal of Research in Personality, 20,* 158–171.

Itil, T.M. & Wadud, A. (1975). Treatment of human aggression with major tranquilizers, antidepressants and newer psychotropic drugs. *Journal of Nervous and Mental Diseases, 160,* 83–99.

Jacobs, P.A., Brunton, M., Melville, M.M., Brittain, R.P., & McClermont, W.F. (1965). Aggressive behaviour, mental sub-normality, and the XYY male. *Nature, 208,* 1351–1352.

James, P., & Mosher, D. (1967). Thematic aggression, hostility-guilt, and aggressive behavior. *Journal of Projective Techniques, 3,* 61–67.

Janowsky, D.S., & Risch, C.S. (1987). Role of acetylcholine mechanisms in the affective disorders. In H.Y. Meltzer (Ed.), *Psychopharmacology: the third generation of progress.* New York: Raven Press.

Jeavons, C.M., & Taylor, S.P. (1985). The control of alcohol-related aggression: Redirecting the inebriate's attention to socially appropriate conduct. *Aggressive Behaviour, 11,* 93–101.

Johansson, G.G. (1981). Neural stimulation as a means for generating standardized threat under laboratory conditions. In P.F. Brain & D. Benton (Eds.), *Multidisciplinary approaches to aggression research.* Amsterdam: Elsevier/North Holland.

Johnson, T.E., & Rule, B.G. (1986). Mitigating circumstance information, censure and aggression. *Journal of Personality and Social Psychology, 30,* 537–542.

Jus, A., Villeneuve, J.A, & Gautier, J. (1973). Some remarks on the influence of lithium carbonate on patients with temporal lobe epilepsy. *International Journal of Clinical Pharmacology Therapy and Toxicology, 7,* 67–74.

Kahn, R.S., van Praag, H.M., Wetzler, S., Asnis, G.M., & Barr, G. (1988). Serotonin and anxiety revisited. *Biological Psychiatry, 23,* 189–208.

Kandel, E., & Freed, D. (1989). Frontal-lobe dysfunction and antisocial behaviour: A review. *Journal of Clinical Psychology, 45,* 404–413.

Kapczinski, F., Curran, H.V., Gray, J., & Lader, M. (1994). Flumazenil has an anxiolytic effect in simulated stress. *Psychopharmacology, 114,* 187–189.

Katz, R. (1976). Catecholamines in predatory behavior: a review and critique. *Aggressive Behavior, 2,* 205–212.

Kelly, T.H., & Cherek, D.R. (1993). The effects of alcohol on free-operant aggressive behavior. *Journal of Studies on Alcohol, Suppl. 11,* 40–52.

Kendell, R.E. (1982). The choice of diagnostic criteria for biological research. *Archives of General Psychiatry, 39,* 1334–1339.

Kennedy, H.G., Kemp, L.I., & Dyer, D.E. (1992). Fear and anger in delusional (paranoid) disorder: The association with violence. *British Journal of Psychiatry, 160,* 488–492.

Kermani, E.J. (1981). Violent psychiatric patients: a study. *American Journal of Psychotherapy, 35,* 215–225.

Kidron, R., Averbuch, I., Klein, E., & Belmaker, R.H. (1985). Carbamazepine-induced reduction of blood levels of haloperidol in chronic schizophrenia. *Biological Psychiatry, 20,* 219–222.

Kimble, G.A. (1989). Psychology from a standpoint of a generalist. *American Psychologist, 44,* 491–499.

Knott, P. (1970). A further methodological study of the measurement of interpersonal aggression. *Psychological Reports, 26,* 807–809.

Kochansky, G.E., Salzman, C., Shader, R.I., Harmatz, J.S., & Ogeltree, A.M. (1975). The differential effects of chlordiazepoxide and oxazepam on hostility in a small group setting. *American Journal of Psychiatry, 132,* 861–863.

Kochansky, G.E., Salzman, C., Shader, R.I., Harmatz, J.S., & Ogeltree, A.M. (1977). Effects of chlordiazepoxide and oxazepam administration on verbal hostility. *Archives of General Psychiatry, 34,* 1457–1459.

Kotler, M., Finkelstein, G., Molcho, A., et al. (1993). Correlates of suicide and violence risk in an inpatient population: Coping styles and social support. *Psychiatry Research, 47,* 281–290.

Kraft, T. (1971). Social anxiety model of alcoholism. *Perceptual and Motor Skills, 33,* 797–798.

Krasner, L., & Ullmann, L.P. (1973). *Behaviour influence and personality.* New York: Holt, Rinehart & Winston.

Krsiak, M., & Sulcova, A. (1990). Differential effects of six structurally related benzodiazepines on some ethological measures of timidity, aggression and locomotion in mice. *Psychopharmacology, 101,* 396–402.

Kuhn, D.Z., Madsen, C.H., & Becker, W.C. (1967). Effects of exposure to an aggressive model and "frustration" on children's aggressive behaviour. *Child Development, 38,* 739–745.

Kulik, J.A., & Brown, R. (1979). Frustration, attribution of blame and aggression. *Journal of Experimental and Social Psychology, 15,* 183–194.

Lader, M.H., & Montagu, J.D. (1962). The psychogalvanic reflex; a pharmacological study of the peripheral mechanism. *Journal of Neurology, Neurosurgery and Psychiatry, 25,* 126–133.

Lagerspetz, K. (1979). Modification of aggressiveness in mice. In S. Feshbach & A. Fraczek (Eds.), *Aggression and behavior change.* New York: Praeger.

Lammers, A.J.J.C., & van Rossum, J. (1968). Bizarre social behaviour in rats induced by a combination of a peripheral decarboxylase inhibitor and DOPA. *European Journal of Pharmacology, 5,* 103–106.

Lamprecht, F., Eichelman, B.S., & Thoa, N. (1972). Rat fighting behavior: serum dopamine-beta-hydroxylase and hypothalamic tyrosine hydroxylase. *Science, 177,* 1214–1215.

Lang, A.R., Goeckner, D.J., Adesso, V.J., & Marlatt, G.A. (1975). Effets of alcohol on aggression in male social drinkers. *Journal of Abnormal Psychology, 84,* 508–518.

Larsen, P.B., Schneiderman, N., & Pasin, R.D. (1986). Physiological bases of cardiovascular psychophysiology. In M.G.H. Coles, E. Donchin, & S.W. Porges (Eds.), *Psychophysiology: Systems, processes and applications.* New York: Guilford Press.

Lazarus, R.S. (1991). Progress on a cognitive-motivational-relational theory of emotion. *American Psychologist, 46,* 819–834.

LeDoux, J.E. (1989). Cognitive-emotional interactions in the brain. *Cognition and Emotion, 3,* 267–289.

Leicester, J. (1982). Temper tantrums, epilepsy and episodic dyscontrol. *British Journal of Psychiatry, 141,* 262–266.

Lesser, I.M., Lydiard, R.B., Antal, E., Rubin, R.T., Ballenger, J.C., & DuPont, R. (1992). Alprazolam plasma concentrations and treatment response in panic disorder and agoraphobia. *American Journal of Psychiatry, 149,* 1556–1562.

Lester, D. (1995). The concentration of neurotransmitter metabolites in the cerebrospinal fluid of suicidal individuals: A meta-analysis. *Pharmaco-psychiatry, 28,* 45–50.

Levanthal, B.L., & Brodie, H.K.H. (1981). The pharmacology of violence. In D.A. Hamburg & M.B. Trudeau (Eds.), *Biobehavioral aspects of aggression.* New York: Liss.

Levenson, R.W., Sher, K.J., Grossman, L.K., Newman, J., & Newlin, D.B. (1980). Alcohol and stress response dampening: pharmacological effects, expectancy, and tension reduction. *Journal of Abnormal Psychology, 89,* 528–538.

Levine, A.M. (1988). Buspirone and agitation in head injury. *Brain Injury, 2,* 165–187.

Light, K.C., & Obrist, P.A. (1983). Task difficulty, heart rate reactivity, and cardiovascular responses to an appetitive reaction time task. *Psychophysiology, 20,* 301–311.

Lindgren, T., & Kantak, K.M. (1987). Effects of serotonin receptor agonists and antagonists on offensive aggression in mice. *Aggressive Behaviour, 13,* 87–96.

Lindzey, G., Loehlin, J., Manosevitz, M., & Thiessen, D.D. (1971). Behavioral genetics. *Annual Reviews of Psychology, 22,* 39–94.

Linnoila, M.I., & Virkkunen, M. (1992). Agopression, suicidality, and serotonin. *Journal of Clinical Psychiatry, 53 (Suppl. 10)*, 46–51.

Linnoila, M.I., De Jong, J., & Virkkunen, M. (1989). Family history of alcoholism in violent offenders and impulsive fire setters. *Archives of General Psychiatry, 46*, 613–616.

Linnoila, M.I., Virkkunen, M., Scheinin, M., Nuutila, A., Rimon, R., & Goodwin, F.K. (1983). Low cerebrospinal fluid 5–hydroxyindoleacetic acid concentration differentiates impulsive from non-impulsive violent behaviour. *Life Sciences, 33*, 2609–2614.

Lorenz, K. (1966). *On aggression*. New York: Harcourt, Brace & World.

Lothstein, L.M., & Jones, P. (1978). Discriminating violent individuals by means of various psychological tests. *Journal of Personality Assessment, 42*, 237–243.

Luchins, D. (1984). Carbamazepine in violent nonepileptic schizophrenics. *Psychopharmacology Bulletin, 20*, 569–571.

Lynch, D.M., Eliatamby, C.L.S., & Anderson, A.A. (1985). Pipothiazine palmitate in the management of aggressive mentally handicapped patients. *British Journal of Psychiatry, 146*, 525–9.

Maccoby, E.E., & Jacklin, C.N. (1974). *The psychology of sex differences*. Stanford, CA: Stanford University Press.

Maccoby, E.E., & Jacklin, C.N. (1980). Sex differences in aggression: A rejoiner and reprise. *Child Development, 51*, 964–980.

Magnusson, D. (1988). *Paths through life, Vol. 1: Individual development from an interactional perspective: A longitudinal study*. Hillsdale, NJ: Lawrence Erlbaum Associates Inc.

Maiuro, R.D., Cahn, T.S., & Vitiliano, P.P. (1986). Assertiveness deficits and hostility in domestically violent men. *Violence Victims, 1*, 279–289.

Maiuro, R.D., Cahn, T.S., Vitiliano, P.P., Wagner, B.C., & Zegree, J.B. (1988). Anger, hostility, and depression in domestically violent versus generally assaultive men and nonviolent control subjects. *Journal of Consulting and Clinical Psychology, 56*, 17–23.

Mandell, A.J. (1978). Towards a psychobiology of transcendance, God in the brain. In. J.M. Davidson & R.J. Davidson (Eds.), *The psychobiology of consciousness*. New York: Plenum.

Mandler, G. (1972). Helplessness: Theory and research in anxiety. In C.D. Spielberger (Ed.), *Anxiety: Current trends in theory and research, Vol. 2*. New York: Academic Press.

Mann, J.J., Stanley, M., McBride, P.A., & McEwen, B.S. (1986). Increased serotonin and beta-adrenergic receptor binding in the frontal cortices of suicide victims. *Archives of General Psychiatry, 43*, 954–959.

Mark, V.H., & Ervin, F.R. (1970). *Violence and the brain*. New York: Harper & Row.

Marks, I.M., Swinson, R.P., Basoglu, M., et al. (1993). Alprazolam and exposure alone and combined in panic disorder with agoraphobia. A controlled study in London and Toronto. *British Journal of Psychiatry, 162*, 776–787.

Markovitz, P.J., Calabrese, J.R., Schulz, S.C., et al. (1991). Fluoxetine in borderline and schizotypal personality disorder. *American Journal of Psychiatry, 148*, 1064–1067.

Marshall, G.D., & Zimbardo, P.G. (1979). Affective consequences of inadequately explained physiological arousal. *Journal of Personality and Social Psychology, 37*, 970–988.

Martinez-Cano, H., Vela-Bueno, A., de Iceta, M., Pomalima, R., & Martinez-Gras, I. (1995). Benzodiazepine withdrawal syndrome seizures. *Pharmacopsychiatry, 28*, 257–262.

Maslach, C. (1979). Negative emotional biasing of unexplained arousal. *Journal of Personality and Social Psychology, 37*, 953–969.

Mattes, J.A. (1990). Comparative effectiveness of carbamazepine and propranolol for rage attacks. *Journal of Neuropsychiatry, 2*, 159–164.

Mattes, J.A., Rosenberg, J., & Maya, D. (1984). Carbamazepine versus propranolol in patients with uncontrolled rage outbursts. *Psychopharmacology Bulletin, 20*, 98–106.

Mazur, A. (1995). Biosocial models of deviant behavior among male army veterans. *Biological Psychology, 41*, 271–293.

McClelland, D.C., Davis, W.N., Kalin, R., & Wanner, E. (1972). *The drinking man*. New York: Free Press.

McCormack, H.M., Horne, D.J., & Sheather, S. (1988). Clinical applications of visual analogue scales: a critical review. *Psychological Medicine, 18*, 1007–1019.

McDonald, R.L. (1967). The effects of personality type on drug response. *Archives of General Psychiatry, 17*, 680–686.

McGregor, A.M., & Herbert, J. (1992). Differential effects of excito-toxic basolateral and corticomedial lesions of the amygdala on the behavioural and endocrine responses to either sexual or aggression-promoting stimuli in the male rat. *Brain Research, 574*, 9–20.

McMillen, B.A., Scott, S.M., William, H.L., & Sanghera, M.K. (1987). Effect of gepirone, an arylpiperazine anxiolytic drug, on aggressive behaviour and brain monoaminergic neurotransmission. *Naunyn Schmiederberg's Archives of Pharmacology, 335*, 454–464.

Mednick, S.A., Brennan, P., & Kandel, E. (1988). Predisposition to violence. *Aggressive Behavior, 14*, 25–33.

Mednick, S.A., Gabrielli, W.F., Jr., & Hutchings, B. (1987). Genetic factors in the etiology of criminal behavior. In S.A. Mednick, T.E. Moffitt, & S.A. Stack (Eds.), *The causes of crime. New biological approaches*. Cambridge: Cambridge University Press.

Mednick, S.A., Pollock, V., Volavka, J., & Gabrielli, W.F. (1982). Biology and violence. In M.E. Wolfgang & N.A. Weiner (Eds.), *Criminal violence*. Beverly Hills, CA: Sage Publications.

Megargee, E.I. (1966). Undercontrolled and overcontrolled personality types in extreme antisocial aggression. *Psychological Monographs, 80(3)*.

Megargee, E.I. (1969). Conscientious objectors' scores on the MMPI O-H (Overcontrolled-Hostility) Scale. *Proceedings of the 77th Annual Convention of the American Psychological Association*. Washington, DC: American Psychiatric Association.

Megargee, E.I. (1970). The prediction of violence with psychological tests. In C.D. Spielberger (Ed.), *Current topics in clinical and community psychology, Vol. 2*. New York: Academic Press.

Megargee, E.I. (1985). The dynamics of aggression and their application to cardiovascular disorders. In M.A. Chesney & R.H. Rosenman (Eds.), *Anger and hostility in cardiovascular and behavioral disorders*. Washington, DC: Hemisphere.

Megargee, E.I., Cook., P.E., & Mendelsohn, G.A. (1967). Development and evaluation of an MMPI scale of assaultiveness in overcontrolled individuals. *Journal of Abnormal Psychology, 72*, 519–528.

Mellerup, E.T., & Plenge, P. (1990). The side effects of lithium. *Biological Psychiatry, 28,* 464–466.

Meltzer, H.Y., & Lowe, M.T. (1987). The serotonin hypothesis of depression. In H.Y. Meltzer (Ed.), *Psychopharmacology: Third generaton of progress.* New York: Raven Press.

Mendoza, R., Djenderedjian, A.H., Adams, J., & Ananth, J. (1987). Midazolam in acute psychotic patients with hyperarousal. *Journal of Clinical Psychiatry, 48,* 291–292.

Meyerson, L.R., Wennogle, L.P., Abel, M.S., et al. (1982). Human brain receptor alterations in suicide victims. *Pharmacology, Biochemistry and Behaviour, 17,* 159–163.

Miczek, K.A. (1987). The psychopharmacology of aggression. In L.L. Iversen, S.D. Iversen, & S.H. Snyder (Eds.), *Handbook of psychopharmacology, Vol. 19: New directions in behavioral pharmacology.* New York and London: Plenum.

Miczek, K.A., Weerts, E.M., & DeBold, J.F. (1993). Alcohol, benzodiazepine-GABA$_A$ receptor complex and aggression: ethological analysis of individual differences in rodents and primates. *Journal of Studies on Alcohol, Suppl. 11,* 170–179.

Milgram, S. (1963). Behavioral study of obedience. *Journal of Abnormal and Social Psychology, 67,* 371–378.

Milgram, S. (1974). *Obedience to authority.* New York: Harper & Row.

Miller, N.E. (1941). The frustration-aggression hypothesis. *Psychological Review, 48,* 337–342.

Millon, T. (1981). *Disorders of personality: DSM-III, Axis II.* New York: Wiley.

Mischel, W., (1968). *Personality and assessment.* New York: Wiley.

Moffitt, T.E. (1990). The neuropsychology of delinquency: A critical review of theory and research. In N. Morris & M. Tonry (Eds.), *Crime and justice, Vol. 12.* Chicago: University of Chicago Press.

Moffitt, T.E. (1993). Adolescence-limited and life-course-persistent antisocial behavior: A developmental taxonomy. *Psychological Review, 100,* 674–701.

Monahan, J. (1981). *The clinical prediction of violent behaviour.* Rockville, MD: National Institute of Mental Health.

Monroe, R.R. (1970). *Episodic behavior disorders: a psychodynamic and neurophysiological analysis.* Cambridge, MA: Harvard University Press.

Monroe, R.R. (1982). Limbic ictus and atypical psychoses. *Journal of Nervous and Mental Disease, 170,* 711–716.

Montgomery, S.A., & Fineberg, N. (1989). Is there a relationship between serotonin receptor subtypes and selectivity of response in specific psychiatric illnesses? *British Journal of Psychiatry, 155 (Suppl.8),* 63–70.

Morand, C, Young, S.N., & Ervin, F.R. (1983). Clinical response of aggressive schizophrenics to oral tryptophan. *Biological Psychiatry, 18,* 575–578.

Mos, J., & Olivier, B. (1987). Pro-aggressive actions of benzodiazepines. In B. Olivier, J. Mos, & P.F. Brain (Eds.), *Ethopharmacology of agonistic behaviour in animals and humans.* Dordrecht: Martinus Nijhoff.

Moss, H.B., Yao, J.K., & Panzak, G.L. (1990). Serotonergic responsivity and behavioral dimensions in antisocial personality disorder with substance abuse. *Biological Psychiatry, 28,* 325–338.

Mowrer, O.H. (1960). *Learning theory and behavior.* New York: Harper & Row.

Moyer, K.E. (1976). *The psychobiology of aggression.* New York: Harper & Row.

Mueller, C.W. (1983). Environmental stressors and aggressive behavior. In R.G. Geen & E. I. Donnerstein (Eds.), *Aggression: Theoretical and empirical reviews, Vol. 2*. New York: Academic Press.

Murdoch, D., Pihl, R.O., & Ross, D. (1990). Alcohol and crimes of violence: Present issues. *International Journal of Addiction, 25*, 1059–1075.

Myers, D.G. (1994). *Exploring social psychology*. New York: McGraw-Hill.

Myrsten, A. (1971). Effects of alcohol on psychological functions. Experimental studies on non-alcoholic subjects. *Reports from the Psychological Laboratories, University of Stockholm, Suppl. 7*.

Nasby, W., Hayden, B., & DePaulo, B.M. (1979). Attributional bias among aggressive boys to interpret unambiguous social stimuli as displays of hostility. *Journal of Abnormal Psychology, 89*, 459–468.

Neppe, V.M. (1983). Carbamazepine as adjunctive treatment in nonepileptic chronic inpatients with EEG temporal lobe abnormalities. *Journal of Clinical Psychiatry, 44*, 326–331.

Neppe, V.M. (1988). Carbamazepine in nonresponsive psychosis. *Journal of Clinical Psychiatry, 49 (Suppl. 4)*, 22–28.

Neppe, V.M. (1990). Carbamazepine in the non-affective psychotic and in non-psychotic dyscontrol. *International Clinical Psychopharmacology, 5 (Suppl. 1)*, 43–54.

Netter, P., Janke, W., & Erdmann, G. (1995). Experimental models for aggression and inventories for the assessement of aggressive and autoaggressive behavior. *Pharmacopsychiatry (Suppl.), 28*, 58–63.

Nickel, T.W. (1974). The attribution of intention as a critical factor in the relation between frustration and aggression. *Journal of Personality, 42*, 482–492.

Nisbett, R.E., & Schachter, S. (1966). Cognitive manipulation of pain. *Journal of Experimental Social Psychology, 2*, 227–236.

Noble, P., & Rodger, S. (1989). Violence by psychiatric inpatients. *British Journal of Psychiatry, 155*, 384–390.

Norden, M.J. (1989). Fluoxetine in borderline personality disorder. *Progress in Neuro-Psychopharmacology and Biological Psychiatry, 13*, 885–893.

Novaco, R.W. (1975). *Anger control: The development and evaluation of an experimental treatment*. Lexington, MA: Heath.

Obrist, P. (1981). *Cardiovascular psychophysiology: A perspective*. New York: Plenum.

Obrist, P.A. (1982). Cardiac-behavioural interactions: a critical approach. In J.T. Cacioppo & R.E. Petty (Eds.), *Perspectives in cardiovascular psychophysiology*. New York: Guilford Press.

O'Callaghan, M.A.J., & Carroll, D. (1982). *Psychosurgery: A scientific analysis*. Lancaster, UK: Medical & Technical Publishing.

O'Leary, M.R., & Dengerink, H.A. (1973). Aggression as a function of the intensity and pattern of attack. *Journal of Experimental Research in Personality, 7*, 61–70.

Olweus, D. (1979). Stability of aggressive reaction patterns in males: A review. *Psychological Bulletin, 86*, 852–875.

Olweus, D., Mattson, A., Schalling, D., & Low, H. (1980). Testosterone, aggression, physical and personality dimensions in normal adolescent males. *Psychosomatic Medicine, 42*, 253–269.

Olweus, D., Mattsson, A., Schalling, D., & Low, H. (1988). Circulating testosterone levels and aggression in adolescent males: a causal analysis. *Psychosomatic Medicine, 50*, 261–272.

Overall, J.E., & Gorham, D.R. (1962). The Brief Psychiatric Rating Scale. *Psychological Reports, 10,* 799–812.

Owen, F., Chambers, D.R., Cooper, S.J., et al. (1986). Serotonergic mechanisms in brains of suicide victims. *Brain Research, 362,* 185–1

Parke, R.D., & Slaby, R.G. (1983). The development of aggression. In P. Mussen (Ed.), *Handbook of child psychology* (4th ed.). New York: Wiley.

Pastore, N. (1952). The role of arbitrariness in the frustration-aggression hypothesis. *Journal of Abnormal and Social Psychology, 47,* 728–731.

Paul, S.M., Rehavi, M., Skolnick, P., & Goodwin, F.K. (1984). High affinity binding of antidepressants to biogenic amine transport sites in human brain and platelet: studies in depression. In R.M. Post & J.C. Ballenger (Eds.), *Neurobiology of mood disorders.* Baltimore, MD: Williams & Wilkins.

Pearson, M., Wilmot, E., & Podi, M. (1986). A study of violent behaviour among inpatients in a psychiatric hospital. *British Journal of Psychiatry, 149,* 232–235.

Peterson, J.B., Rothfleisch, J., Zelazo, P.D., & Pihl, R.O. (1990). Acute alcohol intoxication and cognitive functioning. *Journal of Studies on Alcohol, 51,* 114–122.

Pericic, D., & Manev, H. (1988). Behavioural evidence for simultaneous dual changes of 5–HY receptor subtypes: mode of antidepressant action? *Life Sciences, 42,* 2593–2601.

Pihl, R.O., Peterson, J.B., & Lau, M.A. (1993). A biosocial model of the alcohol-aggression relationship. *Journal of Studies on Alcohol, Suppl. 11,* 128–139.

Pilowsky, L.S., Ring, H., Shine, P., & Lader, M. (1992). Rapid tranquilisation - a survey of emergency prescribing in a general psychiatric hospital. *British Journal of Psychiatry, 160,* 831–835.

Pinel, J.P.J., Treit, D., & Rovner, L.I. (1977). Temporal lobe aggression in rats. *Science, 197,* 1088–1089.

Pisano, R., & Taylor, S.P. (1971). Reduction of physical aggression: The effects of four strategies. *Journal of Personality and Social Psychology, 19,* 237–242.

Pitkanen-Pulkinen, L. (1979). Self-control as a prerequisite for constructive behavior. In S. Feshbach & A. Fraczek (Eds.), *Aggression and behavior change: Biological and social processes.* New York: Praeger.

Planansky, K., & Johnston, R. (1977). Homicidal aggression in schizophrenic men. *Acta Psychiatrica Scandinavica, 55,* 65–73.

Polakoff, S.A., Sorgi, P.J., & Ratey, J.J. (1986). The treatment of impulsive and aggressive behaviour with nadolol. *Journal of Clinical Psychopharmacology, 6,* 125–126.

Pollock, V.E., Briere, J., Schneider, L., Knop, J., Mednick, S.A., & Goodwin, D.W. (1990). Childhood antecedents of antisocial behaviour: Parental alcoholism and physical abusiveness. *American Journal of Psychiatry, 147,* 1290–1293.

Powell, D.A., Milligan, W.L., & Walters, K. (1973). The effects of muscarinic cholinergic blockade upon shock elicited aggression. *Pharmacology, Biochemistry and Behavior, 1,* 389–394.

Pratt, J., Jenner, P., & Marsden, C.D. (1985). Comparison of the effects of benzodiazepines and other anticonvulsant drugs on synthesis and utilization of 5–HT in mouse brain. *Neuropharmacology, 24,* 59–68.

Price, W.H., & Whatmore, P.B. (1967). Behavior disorders and pattern of crime among XYY males identified at a maximum security hospital. *British Medical Journal, 1,* 533–536.

Priest, R.G., Tanner, M., Gandhi, M.D., & Bhandari, S. (1995). Hostility and the psychiatric patient. *American Journal of Forensic Psychiatry, 16,* 21–31.

Puglisi-Allegra, S., & Mandel, P. (1980). Effects of sodium dipropyl-acetate, muscimol hydrobromide and (RS) nipecotic acid amide on isolation-induced aggressive behavior in mice. *Psychopharmacology, 70,* 287–290.

Puglisi-Allegra, S., Simler, S., & Kempf, E. (1981). Involvement of the GABAergic system on shock-induced aggressive behavior in two strains of mice. *Pharmacology, Biochemistry and Behavior, 14 (Suppl. 1),* 13–18.

Pyke, R.E., & Kraus, M. (1988). Alprazolam in the treatment of panic attack patients with and without major depression. *Journal of Clinical Psychiatry, 49,* 66–68.

Quick, M., & Azmitia, E. (1983). Selective destruction of the serotonergic fibers of the fornix-fimbria and cingulum bundle increases 5–HT_2 receptors in rat midbrain. *European Journal of Pharmacology, 90,* 377–384.

Raine, A., Venables, P.H., & Williams, M. (1990). Relationships between central and autonomic measures of arousal at age 15 years and criminality at age 24 years. *Archives of General Psychiatry, 47,* 1003–1007.

Ramani, V., & Gumnit, R.J. (1981). Intensive monitoring of epileptic patients with a history of episodic aggression. *Archives of Neurology, 38,* 570.

Randall, L.O., Schaller, W., & Heise, G. (1960). The psychosedative properties of methaminodiazepoxide. *Journal of Pharmacology and Experimental Therapeutics, 129,* 163–171.

Rasmussen, D.I., Olivier, B., Raghoebar, M., & Mos, J. (1990). Possible clinical applications of serenics and some implications of their preclinical profile for their clinical use in psychiatric disorders. *Drug Metabolism and Drug Interactions, 8,* 159–186.

Ratey, J.J., Sovner, R., Mikkelsen, E., & Chmielinski, H.E. (1989). Buspirone therapy for maladaptive behavior and anxiety in developmentally disabled persons. *Journal of Clinical Psychiatry, 50,* 382–384.

Ratey, J., Sovner, R., Parks, A. & Rogentine, K. (1991). Buspirone treatment of aggression and anxiety in mentally retarded patients: a multiple-baseline, placebo lead-in study. *Journal of Clinical Psychiatry, 52,* 159–162.

Regestein, Q.R., & Reich, P. (1985). Agitation observed during treatment with newer hypnotic drugs. *Journal of Clinical Psychiatry. 46,* 280–283.

Reich, J. (1986). The epidemiology of anxiety. *Journal of Nervous and Mental Disorder, 174,* 129–136.

Reis, D.J. (1974). The chemical coding of aggression in brain. In R.D. Myers & R.R. Drucker-Colin (Eds.), *Neurohumoral coding of brain function.* New York: Plenum.

Renson, G., Adams, J., & Tinklenberg, J. (1978). Buss-Durkee assessment and validation with violent versus nonviolent chronic alcohol abusers. *Journal of Consulting and Clinical Psychology, 46,* 360–361.

Richardson, D. (1981). The effects of alcohol on male violence toward female targets. *Motivation and Emotion, 5,* 333–344.

Robertson, G., Taylor, P.J., & Gunn, J.C. (1987). Does violence have cognitive correlates? *British Journal of Psychiatry, 151,* 63–68.

Rodgers, R.J., & Brown, K. (1976). Amygdaloid function in the central cholinergic mediation of shock-induced aggression in the rat. *Aggressive Behaviour, 2,* 131–152.

Rodgers, R.J., & Waters, A.J. (1985). Benzodiazepines and their antagonists: a pharmacoethological analysis with particular reference to effects on "aggression". *Neuroscience and Biobehavioural Reviews, 9,* 21–35.

Rohsenow, D.J., & Bachorowski, J. (1984). Effects of alcohol and expectancies on verbal aggression in men and women. *Journal of Abnormal Psychology, 93*, 418–432.

Rosenbaum, J.F., Fava, M., Pava, J.A., et al. (1993). Anger attacks in unipolar depression, II: neuroendocrine correlates and changes following fluoxetine treatment. *American Journal of Psychiatry, 150*, 1164–1168.

Rosenbaum, J.F., Woods, S.W., Groves, J.E., & Klerman, G.L. (1984). Emergence of hostility during alprazolam treatment. *American Journal of Psychiatry, 141*, 792–793.

Rosenweig, S. (1981). The current status of the Rosenweig Picture-Frustration Study as a measure of aggression in personality. In P.F. Brain & D. Benton (Eds.), *Multidisciplinary approaches to aggression research.* Amsterdam: Elsevier.

Rosenman, R.H., & Friedman, M. (1974). Neurogenic factors in pathogenesis of coronary heart disease. *Medical Clinics of North America, 58*, 269–279.

Ross, L., Rodin, J., & Zimbardo, P.G. (1969). Toward an attribution therapy. The reduction of fear though induced cognitive-emotional misattribution. *Journal of Personality and Social Psychology, 12*, 279–288.

Rotton, J., Frey, J., Barry, T., Milligan, M., & Fitzpatrick, M. (1979). The air pollution experience and physical aggression. *Journal of Applied Social Psychology, 9*, 397–412.

Roy, A., De Jong, J., & Linnoila, M. (1989). Extraversion in pathological gamblers: correlates with indexes of noradrenergic function. *Archives of General Psychiatry, 46*, 679–681.

Roy, A., Virkkunen, M., & Linnoila, M. (1987). Reduced central serotonin turnover in a subgroup of alcoholics. *Progress in Neuropsychopharmacology and Biological Psychiatry, 11*, 173–178.

Ruedrich, S.L., Grush, L., & Wilson, J. (1990). Beta adrenergic blocking medications for aggressive or self-injurious mentally retarded persons. *American Journal on Mental Retardation, 95*, 110–119.

Rule, B.G. (1978). The hostile and instrumental functions of human aggression. In W.W. Hartup & J. DeWit (Eds.), *Origins of aggression.* The Hague: Mouton.

Rule, B.G., & Hewitt, L.S. (1971). Effects of thwarting on cardiac response and physical aggression. *Journal of Personality and Social Psychology, 19*, 181–187.

Rule, B.G., & Leger, G.J. (1976). Pain cues and differing functions of aggression. *Canadian Journal of Behavioural Science, 8*, 213–223.

Rushton, J.P., Fulker, D.W., Neale, M.C., Nias, D.K.B., & Eysenck, H.J. (1986). Altruism and aggression: The heritability of individual differences. *Journal of Personality and Social Psychology, 50*, 1192–1198.

St. Hilaire, J.M., Gilbert, M., Bouvier, G., & Barbeau, A. (1980). Epilepsy and aggression in two cases with depth electrode studies. In P. Robb (Ed.), *Epilepsy updated: causes and treatment.* Chicago: Yearbook Medical Publishers.

Salzman, C. (1988). Use of benzodiazepines to control disruptive behavior in inpatients. *Journal of Clinical Psychiatry, 49 (Suppl.)*, 13–15.

Salzman, C., Kochansky, G.E., Shader, R.I., Harmatz, J.S., & Ogletree, A.M. (1975). Is oxazepam associated with hostility? *Diseases of the Nervous System, 36*, 30–32.

Salzman, C., Kochansky, G.E., Shader, R.I., Porrino, L.J., Harmatz, J.S., & Swett, C.P. (1974). Chlordiazepoxide-induced hostility in a small group setting. *Archives of General Psychiatry, 31,* 401–405.

Sandberg, A.A., Koeph, G.F., Ishinara, T., & Hauschka, T.S. (1961). An XYY human male. *Lancet, i,* 488–489.

Sanger, D.J., & Blackman, D.E. (1976). Effects of chlordiazepoxide, ripazepam and d-amphetamine on conditioned acceleration of timing behavior in rats. *Psychopharmacology, 48,* 209–215.

Schachter, S., & Singer, J. (1962). Cognitive, social and physiological determinants of emotional state. *Psychological Review, 69,* 379–399.

Schalling, D., & Asberg, M. (1984). Biological and psychological correlates of impulsiveness and monotony avoidance. In J. Strelau, F.H. Farley, & A. Gale (Eds.), *The biological bases of personality and behavior.* Washington, DC: Hemisphere Publishing Corporation.

Schank, R., & Abelson, R. (1977). *Scripts, plans and knowledge.* Hillsdale, NJ: Lawrence Erlbaum Associates Inc.

Schiavi, P.C., Theilgaard, A., Owen, D.R., & White, D. (1984). Sex chromosome anomalies, hormones and aggressivity. *Archives of General Psychiatry, 41,* 93–99.

Schlenker, B.R., & Darby, B.W. (1981). The use of apologies in social predicaments. *Social Psychology Quarterly, 44,* 271–278.

Schultz, S.D. (1954). A differentiation of several forms of hostility by scales empirically constructed from significant items on the Minnesota Multiphasic Personality Inventory. Unpublished doctoral dissertation, Pennsylvania State College. Cited in A.H. Buss (1961), *The psychology of aggression.* Chichester, UK: Wiley.

Schwartz, G.S., Kane, T.R., Joseph, J.M., & Tedeschi, J.T. (1978). The effects of post-transgression remorse on perceived aggression, attribution of intent, and level of punishment. *Journal of Social and Clinical Psychology, 17,* 293–297.

Sellal, F., Danion, J.-M., Kauffmann-Muller, F., et al. (1992). Differential effects of diazepam or lorazepam on repetition priming in healthy volunteers. *Psychopharmacology, 108,* 371–379.

Selmanoff, M., & Ginsburg, B.E. (1981). Genetic variability in aggression and endocrine function in inbred strains of mice. In P.F. Brain & D. Benton (Eds.), *Multidisciplinary approaches to aggression research.* Amsterdam: Elsevier/North Holland.

Shader, R.I., Jackson, A.H., & Dodes, L.M. (1974). The antiaggressive effects of lithium in man. *Psychopharmacologia, 40,* 17–24.

Sheard, M.H. (1971). Effects of lithium in human aggression. *Nature, 230,* 113–4.

Sheard, M.H. (1975). Lithium in the treatment of aggression. *Journal of Nervous and Mental Disease, 160,* 108–18.

Sheard, M.H., Marini, J.L., Bridges, C.I., & Wagner, E. (1976). The effect of lithium in impulsive aggressive behavior in man. *American Journal of Psychiatry, 133,* 1409–1413.

Sher, K.J., & Levenson, R.W. (1982). Risk for alcoholism and individual differences in the stress-response-dampening effect of alcohol. *Journal of Abnormal Psychology, 91,* 350–367.

Sher, K.J., & Levenson, R.W. (1983). Alcohol and tension reduction: The importance of individual differences. In L.A. Pohorecky & J. Brick (Eds.), *Stress and alcohol use.* Amsterdam: Elsevier.

Shortell, J., Epstein, S., & Taylor, S.P. (1970). Instigation to aggression as a function of degree of defeat and the capacity for massive retaliation. *Journal of Personality, 38*, 313–328.

Shuntich, R.J., & Taylor, S.P. (1972). The effects of alcohol on human physical aggression. *Journal of Experimental Research in Personality, 6*, 34–38.

Siegal, S.M. (1956). The relationship of hostility to authoritarianism. *Journal of Abnormal Social Psychology, 52*, 368–373.

Siegal, S.M., Spilka, B., & Miller, L. (1957). The direction of manifest hostility: its measurement and meaning. *American Psychologist, 12*, 421.

Siegel, J.M. (1986). The multidimensional anger inventory. *Journal of Personality and Social Psychology, 51*, 191–200.

Siever, L.J., Coccaro, E.F., Zemishlany, Z., Silverman, J., Klar, H., Losonczy, M.F., Davidson, M., Friedman, R., Mohs, R.C., & Davis K.L. (1987). Psychobiology of personality disorders: Pharmacologic implications. *Psychopharmacology Bulletin, 23*, 333–336.

Sijbesma, H., Schipper, J., & De Kloet, E.R. (1990). Eltoprazine, a drug which reduces aggressive behavior, binds selectively to $5-HT_1$ receptor sites in the rat brain: an autoradiographic study. *European Journal of Pharmacology, 177*, 55–66.

Silver, J.M., Yudofsky, S.C., Kogan, M., & Katz, B.L. (1986). Elevation of thioridazine plasma levels by propranolol. *American Journal of Psychiatry, 143*, 1290–1292.

Silverman, J.M., Pinkhan, L., Horvath, T.B., et al. (1991). Affective and impulsive personality disorder traits in the relatives of borderline personality disorder. *American Journal of Psychiatry, 148*, 1378–1385.

Smith, D.I., & Burvill, P.W. (1987). Effect on juvenile crime of lowering the drinking age in three Australian states. *British Journal of Addiction, 82*, 181–188.

Smith, D.E., King, M.B., & Hoebel, B. (1970). Lateral hypothalamic control of killing: evidence for a cholinoceptive mechanism. *Science, 167*, 900–901.

Soloff, P.H., Cornelius, J.R., George, A., et al. (1993). Efficacy of phenelzine and haloperidol in borderline personality disorder. *Archives of General Psychiatry, 50*, 377–385.

Soloff, P.H., George, A., Nathan, R.S., Schulz, P.M., Ulrich, R.F., & Perel, J.M. (1986). Progress in pharmacotherapy of borderline disorders: a double-blind study of amytriptyline, haloperidol and placebo. *Archives of General Psychiatry, 43*, 91–697.

Soloff, P.H., George, A., Nathan, R.S., et al. (1989). Amitriptyline versus haloperidol in borderlines: final outcomes and predictors of response. *Journal of Clinical Psychopharmacology, 9*, 238–246.

Sorgi, P.J., Ratey, J.J., & Polakoff, S. (1986). β-adrenergic blockers for the control of aggressive behavior in patients with chronic schizophrenia. *American Journal of Psychiatry, 143*, 775–7.

Soubrié, P. (1986). Reconciling the role of central serotonin neurons in human and animal behaviour. *Behavioral and Brain Sciences, 9*, 319–364.

Soubrié, P., Blas, C., Ferron, A., & Glowinski, J. (1983). Chlordiazepoxide reduces in vivo serotonin release in the basal ganglia of "encephale isole" but not of anaesthetized cats: Evidence for a dorsal raphe site of action. *Journal of Pharmacology and Experimental Therapeutics, 226*, 526–532.

Spielberger, C.D., Gorsuch, R.L., & Lushene, R.E. (1970). *The Stait-Trait Anxiety Inventory*. Palo Alto, CA: Consulting Psychologists Press.

Spielberger, C.D., Jacobs, G., Russell, S., & Crane, R.S. (1983). Assessment of anger: The state-trait anger scale. In J.N. Butcher & C.D. Spielberger (Eds.), *Advances in personality assessment, Vol 2*. Hillsdale, NJ: Lawrence Erlbaum Associates Inc.

Spielberger, C.D., Johnson, E.H., Russell, S.F., Crane, R.J., Jacobs, G.A., & Worden, T.J. (1985). The experience and expression of anger: construction and validation of an anger expression scale. In M.A. Chesney & R.H. Rosenman (Eds.), *Anger and hostility in cardiovascular and behavioral disorders*. New York: Hemisphere/McGraw-Hill.

Stanley, M., & Mann, J.J. (1983). Increased serotonin-2 binding sites in frontal cortex of suicide victims. *Lancet, i,* 214–215.

Stanley, M., Virgilio, J., & Gershon, S. (1982). Tritiated imipramine binding sites are decreased in the frontal cortex of suicides. *Science, 216,* 1337–1339.

Steele, C.M., & Josephs, R.A. (1990). Alcohol myopia: Its prized and dangerous effects. *American Psychologist, 45,* 921–933.

Steinmetz, S. (1977). *The cycle of violence: Assertive, aggressive, and abusive family interaction*. New York: Praeger.

Sterling, S., & Edelmann, R.J. (1988). Reactions to anger and anxiety-provoking events: psychopathic and nonpsychopathic groups compared. *Journal of Clinical Psychology, 44,* 96–100.

Stolk, J.M., Conner, R.L., Levine, S., & Barchas, J.D. (1984). Brain norepinephrine metabolism and shock-induced fighting behavior in rats: differential effects of shock and fighting on the neurochemical response to a common footshock stimulus. *Journal of Pharmacology and Experimental Therapeutics, 190,* 193–209.

Stone, M.H. (1993). Long-term outcome in personality disorders. *British Journal of Psychiatry, 162,* 299–313.

Subotnik, L.S. (1989). Men who batter women: From overcontrolled to undercontrolled in anger expression. In G.W. Russell (Ed.), *Violence in intimate relationships*. New York: PMA Publishing Corp.

Tangney, J.P. (1990). Assessing individual differences in proneness to shame and guilt: Development of the Self-conscious Affect and Attribution Inventory. *Journal of Personality and Social Psychology, 59,* 102–111.

Tangney, J.P., Wagner, P., Fletcher, C., & Gramzow, R. (1992). Shames into anger? The relation of shame and guilt to anger and self-reported aggression. *Journal of Personality and Social Psychology, 62,* 669–675.

Tardiff, K. (1981). Emergency control measures for psychiatric inpatients. *Journal of Nervous and Mental Disease, 169,* 614–618.

Tardiff, K., & Sweillam, A. (1980). Assault, suicide and mental illness. *Archives of General Psychiatry, 37,* 164–169.

Tardiff, K., & Sweillam, A. (1982). Assaultive behavior among chronic inpatients. *American Journal of Psychiatry, 139,* 212–215.

Taylor, S.P. (1967). Aggressive behavior and physiology arousal as a function of provocation and the tendency to inhibit aggression. *Journal of Personality, 35,* 297–310.

Taylor, S.P. (1970). Aggressive behavior as a function of approval motivation and physical attack. *Psychonomic Science, 18,* 195–196.

Taylor, S.P., & Chermack, S.T. (1993). Alcohol, drugs and human physical aggression. *Journal of Studies on Alcohol, Suppl. 11,* 78–88.

Taylor, S.P., & Gammon, C.B. (1975). Effects of type and dose of alcohol on human physical aggression. *Journal of Personality and Social Psychology, 32,* 169–175.

Taylor, S.P., & Leonard, K.E. (1983). Alcohol and human physical aggression. In R.G. Green & E.I. Donnerstein (Eds.), *Aggression: Theoretical empirical reviews* (2nd ed.). San Diego, CA: Academic Press.

Taylor, S.P., Schmutte, G.T., Leonard, K.E., & Cranston, J.W. (1979). The effects of alcohol and extreme provocation on the use of a highly noxious electric shock. *Motivated Emotion, 3,* 73–81.

Tedeschi, J.T. (1984). A social interpretation of human aggression. In A. Mummendey (Ed.), *Social psychology of aggression.* Berlin: Springer-Verlag.

Tedeschi, J.T., Gaes, G.G., & Rivera, N. (1977). Aggression and the use of coercive power. *Journal of Social Issues, 33,* 101–125.

Terrell, H.B. (1988). Behavioural dyscontrol associated with combined use of alprazolam and ethanol. *American Journal of Psychiatry, 145,* 1313.

Thoa, N.B., Eichelman, B., & Richardson, J. (1972). 6–Hydroxydopa depletion of brain norepinephrine and the facilitation of aggressive behavior. *Science, 178,* 75–77.

Tieger, T. (1980). On the biological basis of sex differences in aggression. *Child Development, 51,* 943–963.

Tiihonen, T., & Hakola, P. (1994). Psychiatric disorders and homicide recidivism. *American Journal of Psychiatry, 151,* 436–438.

Tiller, J.G. (1988). Short-term buspirone treatment in disinhibition with dementia. *Lancet, 1,* 1169.

Toch, H. (1980). *Violent men* (rev. ed.). Cambridge, MA: Schenkman.

Torgerson, A.M. (1984). Genetic and nosological aspects of schizotypal and borderline personality disorders. *Archives of General Psychiatry, 41,* 546–554.

Torrey, E.F. (1994). Violent behaviour by individuals with serious mental illness. *Hospital and Community Psychiatry, 45,* 653–662.

Traskman, L., Asberg, M., Bertilsson, L., & Sjostrand, L. (1981). Monoamine metabolites in CSF and suicidal behavior. *Archives of General Psychiatry, 38,* 631–636.

Treiman, D.M. (1991). Psychobiology of ictal aggression. In D.B. Smith, D.M. Treiman, & M.R. Trimble (Eds.), *Advances in Neurology 55.* New York: Raven Press.

Trestman, R.L., Coccaro, E.F., Weston, S., et al. (1992). Impulsivity, suicidal behavior, and major depression in the personality disorder: differential correlates with noradrenergic and serotonergic function. *Biological Psychiatry, 31,* 68A.

Tuason, V.B. (1986). A comparison of parenteral loxapine and haloperidol in hostile and aggressive acutely schizophrenic patients. *Journal of Clinical Psychiatry, 47,* 126–129.

Turpin, G., & Siddle, D.A.T. (1983). Effects of stimulus intensity on cardiovascular activity. *Psychophysiology, 20,* 611–624.

Tye, N.C., Everitt, B.J., & Iversen, D.C. (1977). 5–Hydroxytryptamine and punishment. *Nature, 268,* 741–743.

Tye, N.C., Iversen, S.D., & Green, A.R. (1979). The effects of benzodiazepines and serotonergic manipulations on punished responding. *Neuropharmacology, 18,* 689–695.

Tyrer, P. (1988). *Personality disorders: diagnosis, management and course.* London: Butterworth.

Tyrer, P., Rutherford, D., & Huggett, T. (1981). Benzodiazepine withdrawal symptoms and propranolol. *Lancet, i,* 520–522.

Tyrer, P., & Seivewright, N. (1988). Pharmacological treatment of personality disorders. *Clinical Neuropharmacology, 11,* 493–499.

Vale, J.R., & Vale, C.A. (1969). Individual differences and general laws in psychology: a reconciliation. *American Psychologist, 24,* 1093–1108.

Valmier, J., Touchon, J., Daures, P., Zanca, M., & Baldy-Moulinier, M. (1987). Correlations between cerebral blood flow variations and clinical parameters in temporal lobe epilepsy: an interictal study. *Journal of Neurology, Neurosurgery and Psychiatry, 50,* 1306.

Van Goozen, S.H.M., Frijda, N.H., Kindt, M., & van de Poll, N.E. (1994). Anger proneness in women: Development and validation of the anger situation questionnaire. *Aggressive Behavior, 20,* 79–100.

van Praag, H.M., Asnis, G., Kahn, R., et al. (1990). Monoamines and abnormal behavior: a multiaminergic perspective. *British Journal of Psychiatry, 157,* 723–734.

van Praag, H.M., Kahn, R.S., Asnis, G.M., et al. (1987). Desonologization of biological psychiatry or the specificity of 5–HT disturbances in psychiatric disorders. *Journal of Affective Disorders, 13,* 1–8.

van Praag, H.M., & Korf, J. (1971). Endogenous depression with and without disturbances in the 5–hydroxytryptamine metabolism: A biochemical classification. *Psychopharmacology, 19,* 148–152.

Vartiainen, H., Tiihonen, J., Putkonen, A., et al. (1995). Citalopram, a selective serotonin reuptake inhibitor, in the treatment of aggression in schizophrenia. *Acta Psychiatrica Scandinavica, 91,* 348–351.

Velicer, W.F., Govia, J.M., Cherico, N.P., & Corriveau, D.P. (1985). Item format and the structure of the Buss-Durkee Hostility Inventory. *Aggressive Behavior, 11,* 65–82.

Virkkunen, M., Nuutila, A., Goodwin, F.K., & Linnoila, M. (1987). CSF monoamine metabolites in arsonists. *Archives of General Psychiatry, 44,* 241–247.

Volavka, J., Crowner, M., Brizer, D., Convit, A., van Praag, H., & Suckow, R. (1990). Tryptophan treatment of aggressive psychiatric inpatients. *Biological Psychiatry, 28,* 728–732.

Wagner, G.C., Fisher, H., Pole, N., Borve, T., & Johnson, S.K. (1993). Effects of monoaminergic agonists on alcohol-induced increases in mouse aggression. *Journal of Studies on Alcohol, Suppl. 11,* 185–191.

Wartella, E. (1995). Media and problem behaviours in young people. In M. Rutter & D.J. Smith (Eds.), *Psychosocial disorders in young people: time trends and their causes.* Chichester, UK: Wiley.

Wender, P.H., Reimherr, F.W., & Wood, D.R. (1981). Attention deficit disorder (minimal brain dysfuncton) in adults. *Archives of General Psychiatry, 38,* 449–456.

Wender, P.H., Reimherr, F.W., Wood, D.R., & Ward, M. (1985). A controlled study of methylphenydate in the treatment of attention deficit disorder, residual type, in adults. *American Journal of Psychiatry, 142,* 547–552.

White, H.R., Brick, J., & Hansell, S. (1993). A longitudinal investigation of alcohol use and aggression in adolescence. *Journal of Studies on Alcohol, Suppl. 11,* 62–77.

Widiger, T.A. (1992). Categorical versus dimensional classification: implications from and for research. *Journal of Personality Disorders, 6,* 287–300.

Wieck, A. (1996). Ovarian hormones, mood and neurotransmitters. *International Review of Psychiatry, 8,* 17–25.

Wilkinson, C.J. (1985). Effects of diazepam (Valium) and trait anxiety on human physical aggression and emotional state. *Journal of Behavioural Medicine, 8,* 101–114.

Williams, R.B. (1994). Neurobiology, cellular and molecular biology, and psychosomatic medicine. *Psychosomatic Medicine, 56,* 308–315.

Wistedt, B., Rasmussen, A., Pedersen, L., et al. (1990). The development of an observer-scale for measuring social dysfunction and aggression. *Pharmacopsychiatry, 23,* 249–252.

Witkin, H.A., Mednick, S.A., Schulsinger, G., et al. (1976). Criminality in XYY and XXY men. *Science, 193,* 547–555.

Wressell, S.E., Tyrer, S.P., & Berney, T.P. (1990). Reduction in antipsychotic drug dosage in mentally handicapped patients. A hospital study. *British Journal of Psychiatry, 157,* 101–106.

Wyer, R.S., Weatherly, D.A., & Terrell, G. (1965). Social role, aggression, and academic achievement. *Journal of Personality and Social Psychology, 1,* 645–649.

Yen, C.Y., Stangler, R.L., & Millman, N. (1959). Ataractic suppression of isolation-induced aggressive behaviour. *Archives of International Pharmacodynamics, 123,* 179–185.

Yudofsky, S.C., Silver, J.M. & Hales, R.E. (1990). Pharmacologic management of aggression in the elderly. *Journal of Clinical Psychiatry, 51 (Suppl. 10),* 22–28.

Yudofsky, S.C., Silver, J.M., Jackson, W., Endicott, J., & Williams, D. (1986). The overt aggression scale: an operationalised rating scale for verbal and physical aggression. *American Journal of Psychiatry, 143,* 35–39.

Yudofsky, S.C., Silver, J.M., & Schneider, S.E. (1987). Pharmacologic treatment of aggression. *Psychiatric Annals, 17,* 397–407.

Yudofsky, S., Williams, D., & Gorman, J. (1981). Propranolol in the treatment of rage and violent behavior in patients with chronic brain syndrome. *American Journal of Psychiatry, 138,* 218–220.

Zeichner, A., & Pihl, R.O. (1979). Effects of alcohol and behavior contingencies on human aggression. *Journal of Abnormal Psychology, 88,* 153–160.

Zeichner, A., & Pihl, R.O. (1980). Effects of alcohol and instigator intent on human aggression. *Journal of Studies on Alcohol, 41,* 265–276.

Zillman, D. (1978). Attribution and misattribution of excitatory reactions. In J.H. Harvey, W.J. Ickes & R.F. Kidd (Eds.), *New directions in attribution research, Vol. 2.* Hillsdale, NJ: Lawrence Erlbaum Associates Inc.

Zillman, D. (1979). *Hostility and aggression.* Hillsdale, NJ: Lawrence Erlbaum Associates Inc.

Zillman, D. (1988). Cognition-excitation interdependencies in aggressive behavior. *Aggressive Behavior, 14,* 51–64.

Zillman, D., & Cantor, J.R. (1976). Effect of timing of information about mitigating circumstances on emotional responses to provocation and retaliatory behavior. *Journal of Experimental Social Psychology, 12,* 38–55.

Zillman, D., & Johnson, R.C. (1973). Motivated aggressiveness perpetuated by exposure to aggressive films and reduced exposure to nonaggressive films. *Journal of Research in Personality, 7,* 261–276.

Zillmann, D., Baron, R., & Tamborini, R. (1981). Social costs of smoking: Effects of tobacco smoke on hostile behavior. *Journal of Applied Social Psychology, 11,* 548–561.

Zillman, D., Hoyt, J.L., & Day, K.D. (1974). Strength and duration of the effect of aggressive, violent and erotic communication on subsequent aggressive behavior. *Communication Research, 1,* 286–306.

Zuckerman, M. (1987). Is sensation seeking a predisposing trait for alcoholism? In E. Gottheil, K.A. Druley, S. Pashko, & S.P. Weinstein (Eds.), *Stress and addiction.* New York: Brunner-Mazel.

Author index

Subject index

DATE DUE

MAR 0 5 2003			
JAN 0 5 2004			
JAN 1 0 2005			
	WITHDRAW		

Demco, Inc. 38-293